James Benigne

# An Exposition of the Doctrine of the Catholic Church in Matters of Controversie

James Benigne

**An Exposition of the Doctrine of the Catholic Church in Matters of Controversie**

ISBN/EAN: 9783742814449

Manufactured in Europe, USA, Canada, Australia, Japa

Cover: Foto ©Lupo / pixelio.de

Manufactured and distributed by brebook publishing software
(www.brebook.com)

James Benigne

# An Exposition of the Doctrine of the Catholic Church in Matters of Controversie

# AN Exposition

OF THE

## DOCTRINE

OF THE

# Catholic Church

IN

## MATTERS

OF

## CONTROVERSIE.

By the Right Reverend
*JAMES BENIGNE BOSSUET*,
Counsellor to the King, Bishop of *Meaux*, formerly of *Condom*, and Preceptor to the *Dauphin*: First Almoner to the *Dauphiness*.

Done into *English* from the Fifth Edition in *French*.

The Second Edition more Correct.

LONDON, Printed in the Year 1686.

The *Approbation* of the Right Reverend the *Archbishops* and *Bishops*.

WE *have read the Treatise intituled,* An Exposition of the Doctrine of the Catholic Church in Matters of Controversie, Composed by the Right Reverend *James Benigne Bossuet,* Bishop and Lord of *Condom*, Preceptor to his Royal Highness, the Dauphin. *And we declare, That after having examined it, with as much application, as the importance of the matter required, we have found the Doctrine contained in it conformable to the Catholic Apostolic and* Roman *Faith. And therefore we think our selves obliged to propose it, as such, to those whom God has committed to our charge. We are certain, the Faithful will be edified by it, and we hope*

*those*

those of the *Pretended Reform'd Religion*, who read this Work with attention, will receive from it so right an understanding as may conduce to put them into the way of Salvation.

CHARLES MAURICE LE TELLIER, *Archbishop and Duke of* Reims.
CH. de ROSMADEC, *Bishop of* Tours.
FELIX, *Bishop and Earl of* Chalons.
De GRIGNAN, *Bishop of* Usez.
D. DE LIGNY, *Bishop of* Meaux.
NICHOLAS, *Bishop of* Auxerre.
GABRIEL, *Bishop of* Autun.
MARC, *Bishop of* Tarbe.
ARMAND JOHN, *Bishop of* Beziers.
STEPHEN, *Bishop and Prince of* Grenoble.
JULIUS, *Bishop of* Tule.

A

# A Table of Articles contained in this Treatise.

I. Design of this Treatise. Pag. 59
II. Those of the Pretended Reform'd Religion acknowledg, The Catholick Church embraces all the Fundamental Articles of the Christian Religion. 62
III. Religious Worship is terminated only in God. 66
IV. Invocation of Saints. 70
V. Images and Reliques. 78
VI. Justification. 84
VII. Merits of Good Works. 89
VIII. Satisfactions, Purgatory, and Indulgences. 94
IX. Sacraments. 101
    Baptism. 103
    Confirmation. 104
    Penance and Sacramental Confession. ibid.
    Extream Unction. 106
    Marriage. 107
    Holy Orders. ibid.
X. Doctrine of the Church touching the real Presence of the Body and Blood of JESUS CHRIST in the Eucharist,

# The Table.

*rist, and how the Church understands these Words*, This is my Body. 108
XI. *Explication of these Words*, Do this in remembrance of me. 115
XII. *Explication of the Doctrine of the Calvinists, concerning the real Presence.* 119
XIII. *Of Transubstantiation, and Adoration, and in what sense the Eucharist is a Sign.* 135
XIV. *Sacrifice of the Mass.* 137
XV. *Epistle to the* Hebrews. 143
XVI. *Reflections upon the precedent Doctrine.* 149
XVII. *Communion under both Species.* 153
XVIII. *Written, and unwritten Word.* 157
XIX. *Authority of the Church.* 159
XX. *Opinions of the Pretended Reform'd upon the Authority of the Church.* 164
XXI. *Authority of the Holy. S.e, and of Episcopacy.* 176
XXII. *Conclusion of this Treatise.* 177

# AN ADVERTISEMENT

## Upon Account of

## This Present Edition.

ONE would have thought, those of the Pretended Reform'd Religion, in reading this Treatise, should at least have granted, The Doctrine of the Church was faithfully expounded in it. The least they could have allowed a Bishop, was to have understood his own Religion, and to have spoke without disguise, in a Matter, where to dissemble would be a Crime. But, nevertheless, it has fallen out otherwise. This Treatise, whilst a Manuscript, was made use of to instruct several particular Persons, and many Copies of it were dispersed. Upon which the sincerer part of the pretendly Reform'd were almost every where heard to say, That if it were approved, it would in reality take away great Difficul-

### An Advertisement.

ties; But that the Author durst never publish it, and if he should, he would not escape the Censure of all those of his Communion, particularly that of *Rome*, which would not frame it self to his Maxims. After some time, nevertheless, this Book, thus condemned to a perpetual obscurity, appeared ushered in with the Approbation of several Bishops; And the Author, who knew very well he had only expressed in it the Mind of the Council of *Trent*, apprehended not those Censures threatned by the Reformers.

It was not certainly probable the Catholic Faith should be betrayed, in stead of being expounded, by a Bishop; who, after having preached the Gospel all his Life-time, without the least suspicion of his Doctrine, had been newly called to instruct a Prince, whom the greatest King in the World, and the most zealous Defender of the Religion of his Ancestors, causes to be educated in such a manner, that he may be one day one of its principal Supports. But these Gentlemen of the pretended ed Reformation ceased not to persevere in their first Opinion. They expected every moment when Catholics should oppose this Book, and *Rome* it self condemn it.

The occasion of this their imagination was, that the major part, who know nothing of our Doctrine, but as represented to them by their Ministers under the most hideous Ideas, know it not again when shown in its natural Dress. So that it was no hard task to represent the Author of the Exposition to them, as one who mollified the Sentiments of his Religion, and sought out proper and qualifying Moderations to content all Parties.

There has appeared two Answers to this Treatise. The Author of the first would not discover his Name, and till he himself be pleased to declare it, we will not reveal the Secret. It is enough to us, that this Work was approved by the Ministers of *Charenton*, and sent to the Author of the Exposition by the late *M. Conrart*, one endowed with all that Catholics could desire in a Man, excepting a better Religion. The *M. Claude, de Lingle, Daille, & Alix.* other

## An Advertisement.

<small>An. p. 3.
112, 113.
124, 137,
&c.
Nog. p.
63, 94, 95,
109, 110.
An. p. 10.
Nog. p. 40.
Nog. p. 20,
27.
An. Avert.
p. 24.
Rep. p. 3.
An. p. 137.
Nog. p. 24</small>

other Answer was written by *M. Noguier* a Minister, who is amongst them of great repute, and has the esteem of an able Divine. They both pretended the Exposition was contrary to the Decisions of the Council of *Trent*. They both affirm the very Design it self, of Expounding the Doctrine of the Council, to be prohibited by the *Pope*. And they both take care to say, that *M. de Condom* does only mince and extenuate the Doctrine of his Religion. As they represent him, one would think that he relents, that he is coming over to them, that he abandons the Sentiments of his own Church, and embraces those of the

<small>An. Avert.
p. 25, 26,
27, 28, 29.</small>

Pretended Reform'd. In fine, His Treatise agrees not with that Profession of Faith which the *Roman Church* proposes to all those who are of her Communion, and they represent him at defiance with every Article.

If we believe the *Anonymus*, this

<small>An. Avert.
p. 27.</small>

Prelate is come to a fair Composition about *Transubstantiation.* He is willing to content himself with such a Reality of the Body of *JESUS CHRIST*

### An Advertisement.

CHRIST in the Sacrament as the Pretended Reform'd themselves believe. When he treats of the Invocation of Saints, *He endeavours to mitigate and extenuate this Worship of the Roman Church,* both as to her Tenets and Practice. Together with the Veneration of Saints, *he softens that of Images, as also the Articles of Satisfaction, Sacrifice of the Mass, and the Pope's Authority.* As for Images, *he is ashamed of the Excess to which* the Doctrine as well as the Practice has been carried. The *Anonymus,* who represents him as if he had changed the Council of *Trents* Expression in the Article of Satisfaction, will needs have it, that *this change in the Expression proceeds from an Alteration which he introduces in the Doctrine.* In fine, he represents him as one who is going over to the Sentiments of the New Reformation; or, to use his own Expression, *like the Dove which returns to the Ark, not finding where to rest his foot.*

    He not only lays to his charge particular Opinions about the Merits of Good Works, and the Authority
of

*An. p. 24.*

*An. p. 24.*

*An. p. 65.*

*P. 110.*

*An. p. 104, 368.*

of the Pope; but seems ready, if we would conform our selves to the Doctrine of the Exposition, to admit the two Articles which so much perplex those of his Communion.

An Avert. p. 23, 26. Rep. p. 3, &c.
There is nothing generally more frequently repeated in his Book, than the Reproaches he casts upon the Author of the Exposition, for deserting the *Communion of the Church of Rome.*

An Avert. p. 30.
He wishes all those of *M. de Condom*'s Communion would reduce themselves to the Moderations in this Book, and write conformably to its sense. This would (says he a little after) be a happy beginning of a Reformation, which might have much more happy consequences.

Nay more, he takes an advantage from these pretended Alleviations.

An. p. 85.
*These Softnings of M. de Condom (says he) are so far from giving us an ill Opinion of our Reformation, they confirm us that good and moderate Persons themselves condemn (at least a great deal) that we do, and by consequence in some measure acknowledge a Reformation to be useful and necessary.*

He should have concluded quite other-

*An Advertisement.*

otherwise. For a Reformation, such as theirs is, which tends to a change in Doctrine, ought not to regard those things which are condemned already by common consent. But the Pretended Reform'd are willing to persuade themselves, the *Honest* and *moderate Persons* in Communion with *Rome*, amongst which number they allow *M. de Condom* a place, in many things abandon the Sentiments of their Church, and come over as much as they can to the New Reformation.

Thus you see what they are made believe by this strange manner of mis-representing the Catholic Doctrine. Being accustomed to that hideous and terrible Form in which their Ministers represent it in their Pulpits, they imagine those Catholics who lay it open in its natural Purity, disguise and alter it: The more justly we represent it as it is, the less are they acquainted with it; and they imagine we are going over to them, when we only disabuse them of their false Preoccupations.

'Tis true, they say not always the same

same thing. The *Anonymus*, who accuses *M. de Condom* of making such considerable Alterations in the Doctrine of the Church, tells us, *this Exposition has nothing new in it, but a dextrous and delicate turn, and, in fine, nothing but apparent qualifying, which consisting only in some Expressions, or in things of small consequence, gives no body any satisfaction, and only raises new Difficulties, in stead of resolving old.*

P. 61, 62.

So that he seems to be sorry for having represented the Exposition as a Book which made an alteration in the Faith of the Church in all its principal Points, not only in the Expressions, but in the Doctrine.

Let him take it which way he pleases. If he continue to think a Book, so truly Catholic as the Exposition, contrary to so many important Points of the *Roman* Faith, he shows himself never to have had any thing but false Ideas of its Doctrine. And if it be true, that by sweetning only the Expressions, or retrenching, as he says, matters of small consequence, the Catholick Doctrine

*An Advertisement.*

Doctrine seems to him so much more tractable, he will in the end find the Grounds of it were better than he imagined.

But the truth of the matter is, *M. de Condom* has not betrayed his Conscience, nor dissembled the Faith of the Church, in which the Holy Ghost has placed him Bishop; And the Pretended Reform'd could not perswade themselves that a Doctrine which already appears less strange by the sole Exposition of it, and that an Exposition so plain, so easie, and so short, should be that Doctrine which their Ministers represented to them full of Blasphemy and Idolatrous.

We ought, no doubt, to give God thanks for such a disposition, because although it shew in them a strange prejudice against us, yet it gives us hopes they will look upon our Tenets with a more equal temper, when once they are satisfied that the Doctrine of this Treatise, which seems to them already more pleasing, is the pure Doctrine of the Church. So that we are so far from being

being angry at them for making so great a difficulty to believe us when we propose our Faith to them, that we are obliged in Charity to give them Lights so clear and evident, that they may not hereafter doubt but it was faithfully expounded to them. The thing shews it self, and we need but tell them how this Treatise of the Exposition, which they

*An. p. 3.* believe is contrary *not only to the common Tenets of the Doctors of the Roman Church, but also to the words and Doctrine of the Council,* is approved by the whole Church; and that after having received divers Testimonies of Approbation from *Rome,* as well as from other places, it has at last been approved by the Pope himself in the most express and most Authentick manner that could be expected.

This Book had no sooner appeared in publick, but the good repute it had throughout *France* was testified to the Author by Letters from all sorts of People, from Lay-Persons, Ecclesiasticks, Religious, and Doctors, but especially from the most

most Learned Prelates of the Church, whose Testimonies he could even then have produced, had the Subject ben ever so little dubious or new.

But because the Pretended Reform'd are apt to believe us in *France* to have particular thoughts and Tenets which approach nearer theirs in matters of Faith, than the rest of the Church, and particularly than *Rome*: it is convenient we should let them see how matters there were carried on.

As soon as this Treatise was come forth, Cardinal *Bouillon* sent it to Cardinal *Bona*, desiring him to examine it with the utmost Rigour. Letters could no sooner return from *Rome* to *Paris*, but there came also from this Learned and Holy Cardinal, whose Memory will be perpetuated in the Church with eternal Benedictions, that honourable approbation of his, which you will find in the sequel among the rest that we shall speak of.

The Book was Printed the first time about the end of the year 1671.

And

*An Advertisement.*

And this Cardinals anſwer is dated the 26. *January*, 1672.

Cardinal *Sigiſmund*, whoſe death the whole Church doth ſtill regret, writ no leſs favourably concerning it, to *M. l' Abbe de. Dangeau.* He tells us expreſly, that *M. de Condom* has ſpoken very well of the Popes Authority; and whereas this Abbot had written him word, that ſome ſcrupulous perſons here apprehended leſt this Expoſition ſhould be looked upon at *Rome*, as one of thoſe Explications of the Council prohibited by Pope *Pius* IV, he ſhews how ill grounded this ſcruple is. He adds, that he found the Maſter of the Sacred Palace, the Secretary, and the Conſulters of the Congregation *dell' Indice*, all the Cardinals that compoſe it, and in particular the Learned Cardinal *Brancas* Preſident of it, of the ſame opinion, and that they did all of them highly applaud this Treatiſe of the Expoſition. This Letter bears date the 5*th.* of *April*, 1672.

The Reverend Father *Hyacinth Libelli* a famous Divine, whoſe Merits and great Learning raiſed him ſhortly after

*An Advertisement.*

after to the Dignity of Archbishop of *Avignon*, was at that time Master of the Sacred Palace. His Letter of the 26th. of *April*, 1672. written to his E. the Cardinal *Sigismond*, shews what esteem he had of this Book; for he tells him, there is not so much as *the shadow of a fault in it, and that if the Author desire it should be Printed at* Rome, *he will give all the necessary Permissions, without altering the least tittle in it.*

In effect *M. l' Abbe Nazari*, famous for the *Journal des Scavans* which he writes with so much elegance and exactness, was at that time about an *Italian* Version of it, which his E. the Cardinal *de Estrees* caused to be reviewed, and did himself peruse some of the principal parts, that it might be entirely conformable to the original.

The Book had been already done into *English* by the late Abbot *Montague*, whose zeal and vertue is known to the whole World, and there wanted not several Testimonies to shew, that his Version was well received by all the Catholicks of *England*. This Translation was Printed in

*An Advertisement.*

in the Year 1672; and in the Year 1675. it was put into *Irish*, and Printed at *Rome* by the Printers of the Congregation *de Propaganda Fide.*

The Author of this Version, Reverend Father *Porter*, of the Holy Order of St. *Francis*, and Superiour of the Convent of St. *Isidorus*, had some time before ordered a Book called *Securis Evangelica* to be Printed at *Rome* it self, in which a great part of this Treatise of the Exposition was inserted, to prove the Tenets of the Church, when faithfully expounded, are so far from ruining the Foundations of Faith, that they establish them.

In the mean time the *Italian* Version went on with an exactness which became a Subject of that importance, where one Word ill rendred, would spoil the whole Work; and the Reverend Father *Capisucchi*, Master of the *Sacred Palace*, Licensed it to be Printed in the Year 1675, as appears by his Answer of the 27th of *June* following, to *M. de Condom*'s Letter of Thanks for it.

This

## An Advertisement.

This Prelate, after having heard from several parts of *Germany*, how this Treatise had been well approved of there, received a more ample Testimony of it in a Letter of the 27th of *April*, 1673, from the Bishop and Prince of *Paderborn*, then Coadjutor, and at present Bishop of *Munster*; in which that Prelate, whose name bears with it his *Elogium*, says, that he took care this work should be turned into *Latin*, that it might be made Common every where, and especially in *Germany*: but the succeeding Wars, or some other occupations having hindred the performance of it, the Bishop of *Castory*, Apostolical Vicar in the United Provinces, was desirous that a *Latin* Version, which the Author himself had examined, might be made publick, and accordingly it was Printed at *Antwerp* in the Year 1678.

Not long after, in the same Year, by the same Bishop's order, this Treatise was again Printed at *Antwerp* in *Dutch*, with the Approbation of the Ordinary, and the Doctors in those Parts, so very profitable

ble did this Prelate, who composes such excellent things himself, judge this to be for the Instruction of his People.

The Bishop of *Strasbourgh*, who, notwithstanding the miseries of War, was no less careful of his Flock, resolved, about the same time, to procure that this Book might be turned into *High Dutch*, and published with a Pastoral Letter to all those of his Diocess; and having advertised the Pope of his Design, his Holiness caused him to be informed, That *he knew the Book long before; and that as he had heard from all Parts it was the occasion of many Conversions, so the Translation of it could not but be advantageous to his People.*

About this time the *Italian* Version was finished with all the exactness and elegancy possible. Monsieur *l'Abbé Nazari* dedicated it to the Cardinals of the Congregation *de Propaganda Fide*, by whose order it was printed in the same Year 1678. by the Printers belonging to that Congregation.

In the Front of this Version was placed Cardinal *Bona*'s Letter, the
Copy

Copy of which was found at *Rome*, in the Hands of his Secretary, as also the Approbation of *M. l' Abbe Ricci*, Consultor of the Holy Office; of Reverend Father *M. Laurence Brancati de Laurea*, Religious of the Order of St. *Francis*, Consultor and Qualificator of the Holy Office, and Bibliothecarian of the *Vatican*; and of *M. l' Abbe Gradi*, Consultor of the Congregation *dell' Indice*, and Bibliothecarian of the *Vatican*: that is, by the chief Men in *Rome* for Piety and Learning.

This Book was presented to the Pope, as the Latin Translation had been before. And he had the goodness to order *M. l' Abbe de St. Luke* to write to the Author, and to let him know that he was satisfied with it; which he also repeated several times to the *French* Embassador.

The Author, who thought he had nothing more to wish for after such an Approbation, gave, with a profound Respect, his most humble Thanks to the Pope, in a Letter dated *Nov*. 22. 1678. In answer to which, he received a Breve from his Holiness

## An Advertisement.

Holiness of the Fourth of *Jan.* 1679, which contains such an express approbation of this Book, that it cannot be hereafter doubted, but it maintains the pure Doctrine of the Church, and of the Apostolick See.

After this approbation, I needed not to have mentioned any others; but I was willing to shew how this Book, which was threatned by the Ministers with such opposition in the Church, and which they imagined was so contrary to her *common Doctrine,* has naturally (as I may say) passed through all the degrees of Approbation, till it came to that of the Pope himself, which confirms all the rest.

An. Avert. P. 23.
Those of the Pretended Reformed Religion, may at present see how they were imposed upon, when they were told, *The Person was known, and that a Catholick too, who writ against this Exposition of* M. de Condom. It would certainly be a strange thing, this good Catholick, unknown to all others of that Religion, should make the Enemies of the Church

*An Advertisement.*

Church his only Confidents in a Work which he designed against a Bishop of his own Communion. But this Imaginary Writer makes the World stay too long, and the Pretended Reform'd are too credulous, if they suffer themselves hereafter to be amused by such like Promises.

Thus one of the necessary Questions to be answered in vindication of the Exposition is entirely dispatch'd. We need not now go about to refute those Ministers who held the Doctrin of the Exposition not to be that of the Church. Time and Truth have so refuted their allegations, that no room is left for a Reply.

M. *Noguier* would first hear the Oracle of *Rome* speak, before he would admit *M. de Condom* to have rightly explicated the *Catholic Faith. I give p. 41. no credit* (says he) *to those Approbations which these Bishops give in Writing.* Other Doctors want not the like Approbations, and after all, the Oracle of Rome *must speak in matters of Faith.* The *Anonymus* was of the same Mind, and both of them supposed nothing more could

could be said in this matter against *M. de Condom*, if once this Oracle had but spoken. This Oracle has now spoken; this Oracle, I say, which the whole Catholic Church hearkned to with so much respect in the very origine of Christianity; and the Answer it has given, has shewn, that what this Prelate has said, has nothing new, or to be suspected in it; nothing, in a word, which is not receiv'd throughout the whole Church.

Nay, this Question being answered, all the others are in a manner insensibly dispatcht.

*M. de Condom* held, the Catholic Doctrine was never rightly understood by the pretended Reform'd; and that the Authors of their Separation had magnified the Objects to render them odious. What he said, appears now most certain, seeing it is manifest on the one side, the Exposition proposes to them the Catholic Faith, in its Purity; and on the other, that it appeared less strange to them than they thought it was.

But if they find their Pretended Reformers, to the end they might animate

animate them against that Church, in which their Ancestors served God, and in which they themselves received Baptism, were forced to fly to those Calumnies which we see now are not maintainable, how can they dispense with themselves if they search not a new? And why are they not afraid to persist in a Schism, which is manifestly founded upon false Principles, in even the most principal points?

They believ'd, for example, they had good grounds to separate from the Church, under pretence, that whilst she taught the merit of good Works, she destroyed Free Justifica- *Gratuite.* tion, and that Confidence which a Christian ought to have in *JESUS CHRIST* only.

Their breach was principally founded upon this Article. The *Anonymus* thinks it enough to say, An. p. 86. *The Article concerning Justification is one of the chief, that gave occasion to the Reformation.* But M. *Noguiers* speaks more plainly. *Those* (says he) Nog. p. *who were the Authors of our Reforma-* 83. *tion had reason to propose the Article* of *Justification*, as the most principal of the rest, and the most Essential Foundation of their separating. At present then, seeing *M. de Condom* tells them,

*Expos. p. 89, 90.* together with the whole Church, *that she believes we cannot have Life, but in Jesus Christ, in whom alone she puts all her Hope: That she asks all things, hopes all things, and gives thanks for all things, through our Lord JESUS CHRIST: and in fine, that she places all the hopes of Salvation on him:* What would they have more?

*Expos. p. 93.* The Church tells us, *That all our Sins are pardon'd by pure Mercy through JESUS CHRIST, That we owe that Justice which is in us, by the Holy Ghost, to his free undeserved liberality; and that all our good Works which we do, are so many gifts of his Grace.* The Author of this Exposition, who teaches this Doctrine, does not teach it as his own; God forbid.

*Ibid. p. 93.* He teaches it as the clear and manifest Doctrine of the Council of *Trent*; and the Pope approves his Book. After this shall it be again said, That the Council of *Trent*, and the *Roman* Church overthrow Free Justification, and

## An Advertisement.

and that trust which the Faithful ought to repose in *JESUS CHRIST* alone? Is not this unsufferable? And if we should hold our Tongues, would not the Stones cry aloud, and proclaim us injur'd?

It must be also granted, as it was taken notice of in the Exposition, that those Disputes which the Pretended Reform'd have raised upon so capital a Point, are almost brought to nothing, not to say wholly refuted. No body will doubt of it, if they consider what the *Anonymus* has writ concerning the Merit of Good Works with the approbation of four Ministers of *Charenton. We acknowledge* (says he) *as in Justice we must, that* M. de Condom, *and those of the Roman Church, who hold the most Orthodox Opinions concerning Grace, express themselves almost in all things as we do. We agree with them in the main.* But since he promised us so much Justice, he ought to have acknowledged, that M. de Condom, whom he makes here to be of a particular Sect, has not said one word concerning the merit of Good Works,

Ex. p. 93.

An. p. 104.

*An Advertisement.*

Expos. p. 87, 89, 92. 93.

Works, which is not taken from the Council. He said, *Eternal Life ought to be proposed to the Children of God, both as a Grace which is mercifully promised to them by the means of our Saviour Jesus Christ, and as a Recompence which is faithfully rendred to their good Works, and to their merits, in virtue of that Promise.* He said, *That Merits are the gifts of God.* He said, *We can do nothing of our selves, but that we can do all things with him who strengthens us, and that our whole confidence is in JESUS CHRIST.* And the rest, which you may see in their proper place. By this means it is he has satisfied the Pretended Reform'd, and made them say, they agree with him in *the main.* Seeing therefore these Propositions are taken word by word from the Council, they cannot hereafter but acknowledge the *Principal* Subject of their complaints to be taken away, by the sole proposing the Decrees and proper Terms of a Council so much hated and blamed amongst them.

What is it offends them most in the

## An Advertisement.

the Satisfactions which the Church exacts from the Faithful, but only that they think *Catholicks* look upon those of *JESUS CHRIST* as unsufficient? Will they deny their Catechisms, and Confessions of Faith to be grounded upon this foundation? What will they now say, when the Author of the Exposition tells them, with the whole Church, *That JE-SUS CHRIST, God and Man, was solely capable by the infinite Dignity of his Person, to offer up to God a sufficient Satisfaction for our Sins: That this Satisfaction is infinite; That our Saviour has payed the entire Price of our Redemption; That nothing is wanting to this Price, seeing it is infinite; and that the Punishments reserv'd, suffered in Penance, come not from any defect in the Payment, but from a certain Order, which he has established to restrain us, by just fears, and by a saving Discipline?* These and all those other Expressions which make the *Anonymus* say, this Author *extenuates* the Doctrine of Satisfaction, and *returns like the Dove to the Ark*, are the pure Doctrines

Expos. p. 94. & seq.

of the Church, and of the Council of *Trent*, acknowledged for such by the Pope himself. Why therefore will they make People believe the Church looks upon that as an aid to the Satisfactions of *JESUS CHRIST*, which she proposes as a means only to apply it? And with what security of Conscience could the Pretended Reform'd, upon such false suppositions, violate that Holy unity, which *JESUS CHRIST* has so much recommended to his Church?

Expos. p. 116, 117.

They look upon our Sacrifice of the Altar with Horrour, as if *JESUS CHRIST* were again put to Death upon it. What has the Author of the Exposition done to diminish this horror so unjust, but only represented the Doctrine of the Church faithfully? He has told them this Sacrifice is of such a nature, as it admits only a mystical and Spiritual Death of our adorable Victim, who remains always impassible and immortal; and is so far from diminishing the infinite Perfection of the Sacrifice of the Cross, *It is established only to celebrate the remembrance*

brance of it, and to apply the *Vertue*. The *Anonymus* assures us upon this account, that *M. de Condom*, minces the Doctrine of the Catholick Church: And *M. Noguier* also assures us, he has not exposed the Truth. And yet he has only followed the Doctrine of the Council, whose proper Terms he has made use of; and the whole Church approves his Exposition. Who does not therefore perceive how this Doctrine appears to the Pretended Reform'd more moderate and agreeable, only because they do not find those Monsters in it, which they imagine to themselves?

Nog. p. 286.
Ex. p. 141.

The *Anonymus* himself tells us, *The Article of Invocation of Saints is one of the most Essential in Religion*. It is also one of those, wherein *M. de Condom* seems to him *chiefly to soften the Doctrine of his Church*; for he accuses him of it no less than three times. But what has *M. de Condom* said? the same the Catechism of the Council of *Trent* said, the same the Council it self, and the Confession of Faith drawn from it has said, and

An. p. 61.
An. p. 24.
Rep. p. 24, 35.

the

*An Advertisement.*

<small>Expof. p. 71. fequ.</small>

the same which all Catholicks say: *That the Saints offer their Prayers for us*; Is what the Confession of Faith says: *That they offer them by JESUS CHRIST*; is what the Council says: In a word, That we pray to them with the same Mind we pray to *our Brethren, who are upon Earth with us, that is, to Pray with us, and for us, to our common Master, in the name of our common Mediator, who is JESUS CHRIST*. Behold what *M. de Condom* has extracted out of the Council, out of the Catechism, and out of all the publick acts of the Church, the reason his Doctrine has been so much approved.

<small>Expof. p. 71.</small>

This answer is sufficient to ruin the very Grounds of that horrour, which the Pretended Reform'd have conceived against our Doctrine.

<small>Catech. cap. 34.</small>

Their Catechism accuses us of *Idolatry, because by that recourse we have to Saints, we place one part of our Trust in them, and give to them what God has reserv'd to himself.*

But on the contrary, it appears, that when we pray to Saints, we Pray to them only to pray for us; a kind

*An Advertisement.*

kind of Prayer, which by its own Nature, is so far from being reserved to himself by God, who is an independent Being, that it can never be address'd to him.

And if this form of Prayer, *Pray for us*, diminished the trust we have in God, it would be no less condemnable to use it to the living, than to the dead; and St. *Paul* would not have said so often, *Brethren pray for us*. The whole Scripture is full of Prayers of this Nature. 1 Thes. 5. 25. 2. 3. 1. Heb. 13. 18.

But (says their Confession of Faith) this is to overthrow the Mediation of J. C. *who commands us to retire our selves in private, and to pray to his Father in his Name*. How can any one imagine this, seeing neither the Saints, who are in Heaven, nor the Faithful upon Earth, make intercessions by, and through themselves, or in their own Names; but only in the Name of *JESUS CHRIST*, as all Catholicks teach with the Council. Conf. Art. 24. Exp. p. 71.

Thus the Catholick Church has only to declare, as she does, her intention never was to demand any thing

*An Advertisement.*

thing of the Saints, but their humbel Prayers in the name of *JESUS CHRIST*, of like Nature with those the Faithful offer up for one another upon Earth, these few Words will convince for ever the pretendedly Reform'd, of having born her a most unjust hatred.

Nog. p. 36.

But *M. Noguier* declares, *Let M. de Condom say what he will, he will never be perswaded*, the Roman *Church has no other Intention (when she tells us, it is profitable to invocate the Saints) but that we should ask them the assistance of their Prayers, as we do those of the Faithful, who live amongst us.* But what will he say, now he sees the *Roman* Church so visibly approve what *M. de Condom* had in effect only gathered from the universal belief of those in Communion with her? But *why then*, adds *M. Noguier, Do Catholick ask not only the Prayers, but the Aid, Protection, and Succour of the blessed Virgin, and of the Saints?* As if that were not a kind of *Aid, Succour, and Protection*, to recommend the miserable to him, who alone can comfort them.

Nog. p. 37.

them. Such is the Protection we may receive from the blessed Virgin and from the Saints. It is not a small Succour to be aided by their Prayers, seeing they are at the same time so humble, so pleasing, and so efficacious. But why should we argue about words, where the thing is so evident? The Exposition produces to these Ministers most certain Testimonies, by which it is manifest, *that in what Terms soever the Prayers we offer to the Saints be couched, the Intention of the Church, and of the Faithful, always reduces them to this Form, PRAY FOR US.* No matter for that, the Ministers *will never believe it.* They must then raze out of their Catechism, and their Confession of Faith, these accusations of Idolatry, with which they are filled; they must retrench in their Sermons, so many bloody Invectives, which have no other Grounds, and this they cannot resolve of; and let us make what Declarations we can of our Minds, they will neither believe the Council, nor its Catechism, nor our Confession of Faith, nor the

Expos. p. 74.

the Bishops, nor the Pope himself.

Exp. p. 60. It is not necessary to repeat here what is said in the Exposition as to other objections, and principally as to that where they accuse the Church of attributing to Saints a divine Knowledge and Power, whilst she teaches, they can neither know nor do any thing of themselves.

An. Av. p. 24.
Rep. p. 65.
But the accusation of Idolatry has another Foundation, which they accuse *M. de Condom* to have palliated as well as the others. And it is the Article concerning Images, where nevertheless he has searched no other Palliations, but to expose faithfully the meaning of the Church.

There needs no more than this to make the very Suspition of Idolatry to vanish, according to the Principles of the Pretended Reform'd; and they need only in this compare the Doctrine of their own Catechism with that of the Council of *Trent*, represented in the Exposition.

Dim. 23.
Their Catechism upon this Commandment. *Thou shalt not make to thy*

*thy self any Graven Image*, Asks whether God *forbids the making of any Image?* And the answer is, *No, but that God forbids only the making of any Image whereby to represent God or to adore it.* Behold the two things which they think forbidden in this Precept of the Decalogue.

It may be they will do us the Justice to believe we do not pretend to represent God, and that, if they see in some Pictures God the Father Painted in that form which he was pleased so often to appear in to his Prophets, we pretend no more to derogate from his Invisibile and Spiritual Nature, than he himself when he exhibited himself under that form. The Council explicates sufficiently to them upon this account, *that we pretend not* Sess. 25. *thereby to represent or express the Divinity, or to give it any Colours* ; and I think I should do them an injury in proceeding to a clearer Proof.

Let us pass to the second part of their Doctrine, and let us learn from their Catechisms *what form of Adoration*

*tion is condemned.* To *Proſtrate ones ſelf*, ſays the Anſwer, *before an Image, to pray to it, to bow the Knee before it, or ſhew ſome other ſign of reverence, as if God exhibited himſelf there to us.* This is in effect the Errour of the Gentiles, and the proper Character of Idolatry. But they who believe, with the Council, *That Images have neither Divinity nor Vertue in them, for which they ought to be reverenced,* and who place all the benefit, in their recalling the Originals to our remembrance, do not believe that God in them *exhibits himſelf to them.* It is not therefore Idolatry, by the conſent of the Pretended Reform'd, and according to the proper Definition of their Catechiſm.

Expoſ. p. 78, 79, 80, 81, 82 8,

P. 67.

The *Anonymus* ſeems to have been ſenſible of this Truth in that place, where, objecting this Commandment of the Decalogue, he ſays, that God *forbids to make Images, and to worſhip them.* He is in the right. The words of the Precept are expreſs, and the Images there ſpoken of are thoſe which are forbidden to *be made*

*made* as well as to be *worshiped*. That is to say, according to the explication of his Catechism, *those which are made to represent God, and those which are made to show him present*, and which are worshipped with the same intention as full of his Divinity. We neither make nor suffer any of this nature. We do not worship Images; God forbid: but we make use of Images, to put us in mind of the Originals. Our Council, so odious to the pretended Reform'd Church, teaches us no other use of them: Is this then enough to make them say, as that Church doth in her own Confession of Faith, *that all sorts of Idolatry are in vogue in the Roman Church?* Is it for this that her Discipline calls us *Idolaters*, and our Religion *Idolatry?* Without doubt they represent to themselves other things than our Doctrine, when they give us the name of Gentiles: They believe we follow their abominable Errors, and that we believe as they did, that God shews himself to us in those Images.

 Had it not been for these mortal Prejudices,

Art. 28.

Disc. art. 11, 13.
Art. 5. 2.

Prejudices, had it not been for these horrid Ideas which they frame to themselves of the sentiments of the Church, Christians could never have imagined it so detestable a crime to kiss the Cross in remembrance of him who bore our Iniquities upon the wood, nor that so simple and natural a manifestation of those sentiments of tenderness, which that Pious Object excites in our hearts ought to make us regarded as if we Adored *Baal*, or the Golden Calves of *Samaria*.

During this strange preoccupation of the Pretended Reform'd, this Treatise of the Exposition might well appear to them (which really in effect it did) a Book full of Artifice, which did nothing but extenuate the Sentiments of Catholics. But now when they see clearly all the Artifice of this Book is to separate the Doctrines which they have imputed to the Church, from those which she professes, that all the mitigations he makes in Doctrine, is that he has taken off that hideous Masque which the Ministers had put upon

*An Advertisement.* 37

upon it: let them confess this Church was not worthy of so much horror, as they had for her, and that at least she deserves to be heard.

Neither the Pope, nor the See Apostolick ought to be hereafter accused of diminishing that adoration which is due to God, nor that confidence which a Christian ought to establish in his sole goodness through our Lord *Jesus Christ*, since they see, without further search, this Treatise of the Exposition, which is made only to explicate these two Truths, has received at *Rome* and from the Pope himself so Authentic an Approbation.

After this they will certainly be ashamed of that Title which they give the Pope. No one can think on it without horrour, nor hear without astonishment, that the Pretended Reform'd, who boast to follow Scripture word for word, when the Apostle St. *John*, who has alone named Antichrist, tells us three or four times that *Antichrist is he who denies that JESUS CHRIST is come in flesh*, dare so much as think that 2. Joh. 1. 7. 1 Joh. 2. & 4. 3.

he,

he, who teaches so fully the Mystery of *JESUS CHRIST*, that is to say, his Divinity, his Incarnation, the superabundance of his Merits, the necessity of his Grace, and that absolute confidence we must have in it, should nevertheless be that Antichrist described by the Apostle.

But it is objected against the Popes, that they *are that wicked Person, that man of Iniquity who has seated himself in the Temple of God; and makes himself adored as God;* They who confess themselves not only mortal men, but sinners, who pray every day with the rest of the Faithful, *Forgive us our offences,* and who never approach the Altar without Confessing of their sins, and without saying in the most essential part of the Holy Sacrifice, they hope for eternal life, *not by their own Merits, but through the Bounty of God in the Name of our Lord JESUS CHRIST.*

'Tis true, they maintain that Primacy which *JESUS CHRIST* has given them in the Person of St. *Peter*; but it is by That they advance the Work of *JESUS CHRIST* himself, the

2 Thes. 2. 4:

the Work of Charity and Concord which would never have been perfectly accomplished, if the Universal Church and all the *Episcopal* Order had not one Head of Ecclesiastical Government upon Earth, to make the Members act in concurrence, and accomplish in the whole Body the Mystery of Unity so much recommended by the Son of God. It is just as much as nothing to answer, that the Church has her true Head in Heaven, who Unites her by animating her with his Holy Spirit: Who doubts of it! But who does not know this Holy Spirit, who disposes all things with as much sweetness as efficacy, knows also how to prepare exteriour means proportionable to his designs? The Holy Ghost both teaches and governs us interiourly: therefore he establishes Pastors and Teachers to Act exteriourly. The Holy Ghost Unites the Body of the Church, and the Ecclesiastical Government: therefore it is he places at the head a common Father, and a principal disposer, who may Govern the whole Family of *JESUS CHRIST.*

*An Advertisement.*

CHRIST. We will call to witness the Consciences of those of the Pretended Reform'd Religion. In this unfortunate age, when so many wicked Sects endeavour by little and little to undermine the Foundations of Christianity, and believe it enough only to name *JESUS CRHIST* to introduce indifferency in Religion, and manifest impiety into the bosom of the Church, Who sees not the necessity of a Pastor, who may watch over his flock, and, authorized from above, encite all others whose vigilance might slacken? Let them in reality tell us, if it be nor the *Socinians*, the *Anabaptists*, the *Independents*, those who under the name of Christian Liberty would establish indifferency in Religions, and so many other pernicious Sects, which they condemn as well as we, who fly with the greatest impetuosity against St. *Peters* Chair, and cry loudest that his Authority is Tyrannical? I do not wonder at it: Those who would divide the Church, or surprise her, fear nothing more than to see her march against them like a well ranged

## An Advertisement.

ged Army under one Head. Let us not raise a quarrel with any, let us only reflect whence come those Books, wherein these dangerous Licenses, and Antichristian Doctrines are taught: at least none can deny but the See of *Rome*, by the very Constitution of it, is incompatible with these Novelties; and if we could not know by the Gospel that the Primacy of this See is necessary for us, Experience it self would convince us of it. Moreover, we must not be astonished if this Author of the Exposition, who places the essential Authority of this See in those things wherein all Catholic Schools agree, hath been approved without difficulty. The Chair of *St. Peter* stands in need of no disputing; what all Catholics acknowledg without contestation, suffices to maintain that Power which was given to it for edification, and not for destruction. The Pretended Reform'd should hereafter give way no more to those vain Phantoms with which they are frighted. What does it profit them to search in Histories for the Vices of Popes? when

it

if what they meet with there should be true, does the Vices of Men destroy the Institution of *JESUS CHRIST*, and the Privilege of *St. Peter?* Shall the Church rise in Rebellion against a Power which maintains her Unity, under pretense that some have abus'd it? Christians are accustomed to reason upon higher and more true Principles, and know that God is able to maintain his Works in the midst of all the Evils which accompany humane Frailty.

We do then conjure those of the Pretended Reform'd Religion, by that Charity, which is God himself, by the Name of Christian, which is common to us both, not to judge of the Doctrine of our Church, by what they hear in their Sermons or read in their Books, where many times the heat of dispute, and Prevention (not to mention any other) make things frequently otherwise represented then they are; but to hearken to this Exposition of the Catholic Doctrine. It is a work in reality, which consists not so much in disputing, as in explicating clearly our Belief;

*An Advertisement.*

Belief; In which to see how plainly the Author has proceeded, we need only consider his design.

He promised in the very beginning,

1. To propose the true Tenets of the Catholic Church, *and to distinguish them from those which are falsely imputed to her.* Exp. p. 60.

2. To the end no one should doubt but that he faithfully proposed the true Sentiments of the Church, he promised to take them *from the Council of Trent*, where the Church has spoken decisively upon the things in question. Exp. p. 61.

3. He promised to propose to the Pretended Reform'd not all points in general, but *those which caused the greatest separation betwixt them and us*, and, to speak properly, those which they made the occasion of their breach. Exp. p. 60.

4. He promised that what he *said, to make the Decisions of the Council more intelligible, should be approved of in the Church, and manifestly conformable to the Doctrine of the same Council.* Exp. p. 61.

All this is plain and just. And, in the first place, no body can think it strange,

strange we should distinguish the Churches Tenets *from those which are falsely imputed to her*. When Persons are animated beyond measure, for want of a right understanding, and when strange prejudices move great disputes, there is nothing more natural, nothing more charitable, then to explicate matters clearly. The Holy Fathers practised a way fraudless and calm like this, to set men right again. Whilst the *Arians* and *Semi-Arians* decryed the Symbol of *Nice*, and the Consubstantiality of the Son, by the false Ideas they fixed upon them, *St. Athanasius* and *St. Hilarius*, the two most illustrious defenders of the *Nicene* Faith, represented to them the true sense of the Councils: and *St. Hilarius* said to them : *Let us both together condemn false Interpretations, but not destroy the certainty of Faith*——The Word *Consubstantial may be misunderstood : let us resolve how we may rightly understand it*——*We may lay down the true state of Faith betwixt us, if we do not overthrow what has been rightly established, but remove misunderstanding.*

S. Hil. lib. de syn.

*An Advertisement.*

It is Charity it self which dictates such words, and suggests such means to reunite our minds. We may say the same to these of the Pretended Reform'd Religion: If the Merit of Good Works, if Prayers addressed to Saints, if the Eucharist, if the humble satisfactions of Penitents, who endeavour to appease the wrath of God in voluntarily revenging upon themselves by Laborious Exercises his offended Justice, if the Terms we use of a Tradition which claims its Origin from the first Ages, for want of being rightly understood offend you; The Author of the Exposition offers himself to give you the plain and natural explication of them, which the *Church* has always faithfully conserv'd. He says nothing of his own, he alledges not particular Authors; and to the end he may not be suspected of changing the Tenets of the Church, he uses the proper Terms of the Council of *Trent*, where she has explicated her self upon these matters in question: what can there be more rational?

This was the second thing he promised, and he has in this only followed the Example of the Pretended Reform'd. They complain as well as we, their Doctrines are not rightly understood; and the means they propose to come to a true knowledge of them, is not different from that which *M. de Condom* makes use of. Their Synod of D:rt requires that *none judge of the Faith of their Churches from Calumnies picked up here and there, or passages of particular Authors, which are often falsely cited, or wrested to a sense contrary to their Intentions; but from the Confessions of Faith of their Churches, and from the Declaration of their Orthodox Doctrine unanimously made in this Synod.*

*Conclusio Synodi Dordrac. in Syntag. Confess. Fidei edit. Genev. p. 2.*

The Faith then of a Church must be learnt from its publick Definitions, and not from Private Authors, who may be falsely quoted, mis-understood, and may also themselves mis-explicate the Sentiments of their Religion. Upon which account it will be only necessary, that, to expound ours to the Pretended Reform'd, we produce the Decisions of the Council of *Trent*.

I know the very name of this Council

## An Advertisement.

Council offends those of the Reformation, and the *Anonym* is often shews his ill humour against it. But what do his Invectives avail him? We go not here about to justifie the Council: It suffices for this Author of the Exposition, that the Doctrine of this Council is universally received, without Contestation, through the whole Catholic Church, and that she admits of no other Decisions, in these matters of Controversie, but of this Council.

The Pretended Reform'd have always endeavoured to have these Decisions thought ambiguous, and the *Anonymus* reproaches us also with their being capable of a *double or triple sense*. Those who have not read this Council, unless it were in the Invectives of their Ministers, and in the History of *Fa. Paul*, the declared Enemy of it, believe them such: but one word will satisfie them. It is very true, there was some Points the Council would not decide, and they were those concerning which there was no settled Tradition, and which were disputed of in the Schools; It was but reasonable they should be left undecided:

An. p. 11, 12.

*An Advertisement.*

cided: but for those it has decided, it has spoken so precisely, that amongst so many Decrees of this Council produced in the Exposition, the *Anonymus* could not find so much as one, in which there was this double or triple sence he objects against us.

In effect, It is but reading them, and one shall see how they have not any ambiguity, and that it is impossible for men to explicate themselves more clearly.

We may put the Exposition it self to the same Test, and judge by that, whether the *Anonymus* had reason to upbraid the Author of this Exposi-

Avert. p. 25.
Rep. p. 12.

tion with *those rambling and general Terms in which* (says he) *he entanglingly wraps up the most difficult matters.*

The third thing the Author of the Exposition promised, was to treat of those matters *which gave occasion to the Separation.* This is precisely what ought to be done. There is no one who knows not that in disputes there are always some certain principal points upon which mens minds are fixed. It is to these a Person must apply

apply himself who would make it his business to end or appease those contests. Thus did the Author of the Exposition, who in the very beginning declared to the Pretended Reform'd, that he would expound to them those points *from which they took the Subject of their separation.* And to shew it was a deliberate Expression, he again declares the same at the latter end, *that to keep himself fixed to what is principal, he omitted some questions which they of the Pretended Reform'd Religion did not look upon as a lawful Subject of separation.* Exp. p. 60.
Expos. p. 175, 176.

He has kept his word most faithfully, and the Titles alone of the Exposition will make it appear, how he has not omitted any one of those principal Articles.

So that the *Anonymus* should not have accused *M. de Condom* of having *some select Terms to avoid the difficulties which give him the most trouble; of leaving many questions untouched, and making haste to that of the Eucharist, where he thought he could enlarge himself with less disadvantage.* Avert. p. 22.
Repl. p. 168.

What an Idea would he give us of this

this Book of the Exposition! but it destroys it self. Every one sees it was *M. de Condom*'s business to enlarge himself upon that point of the Eucharist, not because he thought he could do it *with less disadvantage*, but because this point is in reality the most difficult, and full of great questions. So that it will appear he has treated these matters with less or greater scope, according as they appear'd less or more embroiling, not to him, but to those, for whom he writes. And if it be true that *he lays aside those difficulties which give him the most trouble*, it must be allow'd, those which give him the least, are in reality those which are the most essential, and those in which the Pretended Reform'd always thought themselves the most secure. He has treated of the worship due to God, of Prayers to Saints, of the honour we render to them, as also to their Images and Reliques. He has spoken of justifying Grace, of the Merit of Good Works, of the necessity of Works, of Satisfaction, of Purgatory, of Indulgences, of Sacramental Confession and
Absolution,

Absolution, of the Real Presence of the Body and Blood of our Saviour in the Eucharist, of that Adoration which is therein due to him, of Transubstantiation, and the Sacrifice of the Altar, of Communion under one Species, of the Authority of Tradition and that of the Church, of the Divine Institution of the Popes Primacy, where he has in one word explained what is to be believed of Episcopacy. He has expounded all these difficulties, and there needs only a little honesty to grant he has been so far from avoiding difficulties, as the *Anonymus* would have it thought, that he has principally applied himself to those which the Pretended Reform'd find the greatest. The *Anonymus* himself tells us *the Invocation of Saints is one of the most essential Articles of Religion*; and at the same time he adds, *this is one of those upon which* M. de Condom *has been most prolix*. What points are more exactly treated in the Exposition than those of the Eucharist and the Sacrifice, that of Images, of Merit, of Good works, of Satisfaction? And is it not in these the Pre-

p. 61.

tended

tended Reform'd find the greatest difficulties. In fine, we will ask even themselves, whether it be not true, that if they were satisfied in all those points treated of in the Exposition, they would not any longer hesitate to embrace the Faith of the Church? It is therefore certain, the Author has treated all those Capital points upon which both of us agree the greatest difficulties move. Nay more, he has always fixed himself to the principal knot of the difficulty, seeing he applies himself chiefly, according to his first promise, to those parts where the Catholic Doctrine is accused to strike at the Foundations of Faith and Christian Piety. It is not therefore to avoid difficulties, he has left some questions untouched which are but Consequences and fuller Explications of those which he has handled, or at least, are such as disturb no body. But, on the contrary, he has done it to the end he might apply himself with less distraction to the chief difficulties upon which depend the Decision of our Controversies.

The Author of the Exposition has been

*An Advertisement.* 53

been no less Faithful in performance of his fourth promise, which was to affirm nothing to make the Council to be better understood, *which was not manifestly conformable to it, and approved of in the Church.*

The *Anonymus* looks upon these words, and all the design of the Exposition, as a *Testimony* which shows the Doctrine of the Roman Church (tho' explained so clearly, and decided in the Council of Trent) *not yet to be so clear, but that it needs an explication.* Exp. p. 61.
An. rep. p. 11.

M. *Nogier* seems also to draw the same Consequence, and they have both of them looked upon the Exposition as an explication which the obscurity of the Council stood in need of. Nog. p. 39, 40.

But we know how the obscurity of a Decision, especially in matters of Faith, is not always that which makes it to be taken in a wrong sense: it is a preoccupation of mind, the ardour of dispute, the heat of Persons engaged, which make them not understand one another, and often attribute to an adversary what he believes the least. So that when the Author of the

Exposition

Exposition proposes the Decisions of the Council of *Trent* to the Pretended Reform'd, and adds what may be useful to remove those Impressions which hinder them from understanding them aright, they ought not to conclude from thence that the Decisions are Ambiguous, but only that nothing is so well digested, nor so clear but may be understood amiss, when prejudice and passion interpose.

An, p. 10.
Nog. p.
40.

To what purpose then do *M. Noguier* and the *Anonymus* object to the Author of the Exposition the Bull of Pope *Pius* IV. The design of the Exposition has nothing of those Glosses, and Commentaries which with great reason this Pope Condemned. For what did those Commentators and Glossars, especially those who have writ Glosses upon the Laws? what did they for the most part but fill the margents with their own imaginations, which most commonly serve only to confound the Text, and which, notwithstanding they give for the Text it self? Let us add, that, for the conservation of Unity, this Pope was obliged not to permit every Doctor

### An Advertisement. 55

ðor to propose decisions upon doubts which succeeding time and vain subtilties might give birth to. Nor has any thing of this nature been done in the Exposition. It is one thing to interpret what is obscure and doubtful, another to propose what is clear, and to make use of it to remove false impressions. The last is what the Author of the Exposition has endeavour'd precisely. And if he have added some of his own Reflexions to the Decisions of this Council, to make them more intelligible to those people who would never look upon them without prejudice, it is because their preoccupation had need of such an assistance.

But why should we speak any more of a thing which is clear enough? We have, in few words given a certain method to enlighten the understandings of those who are the most zealous to maintain this ambiguity of the Council. They need only read in this Exposition its Decrees which are there produced, and convince themselves by their own eyes.

The

The most important thing here, is, that the Author of the Expofition was not deceived when he promifed what he fhould fay, for the better underftanding of this Council, fhould be mainfeftly of the fame Spirit, and approved of in the Church. The matter is in it felf clear, and the following Approbations will make it apparent.

It muft not therefore be fuppos'd henceforwards that the Sentiments explained in this Work, are the *qualifying or the extenuating thoughts* of one man; but the Common Doctrine which we fee is, for this reafon, univerfally approved. It will not therefore avail *M. Noguires* nor the *Anonymus* any thing after this, either to object to us thofe Practices which they call general, or the particular opinion of Doctors. For without examining thefe unneceffary things, it fuffices in one word to fay, that thofe Practifes and Opinions, be they what they will, which are not found to be conformable to the intent and Decifions of the Council, are nothing to Religion, nor to the body of the Catholic

An. p. 2. &c. Nog. 38, &c.

*An Advertisement.* 57

tholic Church, nor ought by conse- Exp. p. 61.
quence, as the Pretended Reform'd Daille A-
do themselves avouch, to give the pol. c. 6. p. 8.
least pretence to separate from us,
because no one is obliged either to
approve or follow them.

But, say they, those abuses ought
to be suppressed: as if one of the ways
to suppress them were not to shew the
truth in its purity without prejudice
to the other means, with which Prudence
and Zeal may inspire the Bishops.
As for the remedy of Schism
practised by the pretended Reformers,
if it were not detestable in it self,
the miseries which it has caused, and
does at present cause throughout
Christendom, would give us a horrour of it.

I will not here reproach the Pretended
Reform'd with the abuses
which are amongst them. This work
of Charity does not permit such like
Recriminations. It suffices I advertise
them that to attaque us in reality,
they must combat, not those abuses
which we Condemn as well as they,
but the Doctrines which we maintain.
But if, in examining them more
                              narrowly,

narrowly, they find, they give not scope enough to their Invectives, they ought at last to acknowledge, we have reason to tell them the Faith which we profess is less worthy of blame than they believed it was.

It remains at present, that we beg of God to grant they may read a Work without bitterness, which is published only to instruct them. The Success is in his Hands who alone can touch the Heart. He knows the Limits he has fixt to the Progress of Errour, and the Miseries of his afflicted Church, by the loss of so great a number of her Children. But we cannot hinder our selves from hoping some great effects towards the reunion of Christians, under a Pope, who exercises so piously, and with so perfect a Zeal, free from Interest, the most holy Function in the World; and under a King, who prefers before all the Conquests that have enlarged his Kingdom, those that might gain him his own Subjects to the Church.

# AN EXPOSITION OF THE DOCTRINE OF THE CHURCH IN MATTERS of CONTROVERSIE.

## SECT. I.

*The Design of this Treatise.*

AFter a Contestation, for above an Age, with those of the Pretended Reform'd Religion; Matters from whence they took the ground of their Separation ought to be sufficiently cleared, and their minds disposed to a right conception of the Sentiments of the Catholic Church. So that to me nothing seems more proper, then to propose her Tenets plainly,

plainly, and simply, and to distinguish them right from those which have been falsly imputed to her. In effect, I have, upon several occasions, taken notice, that the aversion which these Gentlemen have to most of our Sentiments, is grounded upon some false *Ideas*, which they have formed to themselves, concerning them; or else, upon some certain words, which are so offensive to them, that they immediately stop there, and never come so far as to consider the grounds of things. Upon which account, I thought nothing could be more beneficial, than to explicate to them what the Church has defined in the Council of *Trent* concerning those points, which keep them at farthest distant from us; without medling with that which they are accustomed to object either against particular Doctors, or against those Tenets which are neither necessarily, nor universally received. For all Parties agree, and *M. Daille* himself, is of this Opinion, that *it is a very unreasonable thing to attribute the Sentiments of particular Persons to a whole body;*

*Apol. 1.6.*

*The Design of this Treatise.*

body; and he adds, that no separation ought to be but upon the account of Articles authenticly established, to the belief and observance of which all Persons are obliged. I will not meddle then with any thing but the Decrees of the Council of *Trent*; because in them the Church has given her Decision upon these matters now in agitation: and what I shall say, for the better understanding of those Decisions, shall be what is approved of in the Church, and shall manifestly appear conformable to the Doctrine of this Council.

This Exposition of our Doctrine will produce two good effects. The *first*, that many disputes will wholly vanish, because it will appear they are only grounded upon some erroneous explications of our belief. The *second* that those disputes, which remain, will not appear, according to the Principles of the Pretended Reform'd, so Capital, as at first they endeavoured to represent them; and that, according to the same Principles, they contain nothing any ways injurious to the grounds of Faith.

SECT.

## SECT. II.

*Those of the Pretended Reform'd Religion acknowledg, That the Catholic Church embraces all the Fundamental Articles of the Christian Religion.*

ANd to begin with the fundamental and principal Articles of Faith; these Gentlemen of the Pretended Reform'd Religion must of necessity acknowledg they are believed and professed in the Catholic Church.

If they will have them to consist in believing, we must adore one only God, the Father, Son, and Holy Ghost, and that we must put our trust in God alone, through his Son, who became man, was Crucified, and rose again for us; they know in their Consciences we profess this Doctrine: and if they add those other Articles which are comprehended in the Apostles Creed; they do not doubt also but we receive them all without exception, and have a pure

and

*acknowledged by the* Romanists.  63

and true knowledge of them.

*M. Daille* has writ a Treatise, intituled *Faith founded upon the Scriptures*, in which after having exposed all the Articles of Faith held by the Pretended Reform'd Churches, he tells us, *they are beyond all contestation; that the* Roman *Church professes to believe them; that in reality they do not hold all our Opinions, but that we hold all their Articles of Faith*. Part.3.c.1.

This Minister then cannot, unless he destroy his own Faith, deny but that we believe all the principal Articles of the Christian Religion.

But tho' *M. Daille* had not granted thus much, the thing is manifest in it self, and all the world knows, that we believe all those Articles which *Protestants* call Fundamental; so that sincerity it self demands they should without dispute grant us not to have really rejected any of them.

The Pretended Reform'd, who see the advantages we may draw from this acknowledgment, are desirous to deprive us of them, by saying that we destroy those Articles,

*All Fundamental Articles*

ticles, by interposing others contrary to them. This is what they endeavour to perswade by Consequences drawn from our Doctrine; but the same *M. Daillé* (whose authority I alledge once more, not so much to convince them by the Testimony of one of their most Learned Ministers, as because what he says is in it self evident) tells them what they ought to think of such kind of Consequences, supposing ill ones might be drawn from our Doctrine. See what he writes in his Letter to *M. Monglat*, upon account of his Apologie. *Altho' the Opinion of the Lutherans as well as that of Rome does, according to us, infer the destruction of the Humanity of* JESUS CHRIST, *yet this Consequence cannot be attributed to them without Calumny, seeing they do formally reject it.*

There is nothing more essential to the Christian Religion, then the reality of the Human Nature in *JESUS CHRIST*: and yet tho' the Lutherans hold a Doctrine, from whence is inferred the destruction of this

*acknowledged by the* Romanists. 65

this Capital verity, by Consequences, which the Pretended Reform'd judg evident; yet they have not scrupled to offer to Communicate with them; because their Opinion *has no poyson in it*, as *M. Daille* tells us in his A- Cap. 7. pologie; And their Naional *Synode*, held at *Charenton* 1631, admits them *to the Holy Table*, upon this ground, *that they agree in the principal and Fundamental points of Religion.* It is then a certain Maxim establiſhed a-mongſt them, that they muſt not in theſe caſes look upon the Conſequences, which may be drawn from a Doctrine, but purely upon what he propoſes and acknowledges, who teaches it.

So that when they infer by Conſequences, which they pretend to draw from our Doctrine, that we do not ſufficiently acknowledg that Soveraign Glory which is due to God, nor the quality of Saviour and Mediator in *JESUS CHRIST*, nor the infinite value of his Sacrifice, nor the ſuperabundant Plenitude of his Merits: we may defend our ſelves without difficulty from
ſuch

such Consequences, by this short answer of *M. Daille*, and tell them that the Catholic Church disavowing them, they cannot be imputed to her *without Calumny*.

But I will go yet further, and show these Gentlemen of the Pretended Reform'd Religion, by the sole Exposition of our Doctrine, that the Catholic Church is so far from ruining the Fundamental Articles of Faith, either directly or indirectly; that on the contrary she establishes them after so solid and evident a manner, that no one can question her right understanding of them without great injustice.

### SECT. III.

*Religious Worship is terminated in God alone.*

TO begin with that Adoration which is due to God alone; the Catholic Church teaches us, that it consists principally, in believing he is the Creator and Lord of all things, and in adhering to him with all the Powers of our Soul, by Faith, Hope and Charity, as to him alone

*terminates in God alone.*

alone who can render us happy by the Communication of an infinite Good, which is himself.

This interior Adoration, which we render to God in Spirit and in Truth, has its exterior marks, of which the principal is Sacrifice, which cannot be offered to any but to God; because a Sacrifice is established to make a public acknowledgment, and a solemn protestation of Gods Soveraignity, and our absolute dependance.

The same Church teaches us, that all *Religious worship* ought to terminate in God as its necessary end; and that if the honour which she renders to the Blessed Virgin, and to the Saints may, in some sence, be called *Religious*, it is for its necessary relation to God.

But before we explicate any further in what this honour consists, it will not be unuseful to take notice, how those of the Pretended Reformation (obliged by the strength of truth) begin to acknowledg the custom of praying to Saints, and honouring their *Reliques* was established

D even

*Religious Worship*

even in the fourth age of the *Church*. *Monsieur Daille* grants thus much, in that Book he published against the Tradition of the *Latin Church* about the object of Religious Worship, and accuses St. *Basil*, St. *Ambrose*, St. *Hierome*, St. *John Chrysostom*, St. *Augustin*, and many more of those famous Lights of Antiquity who lived in that Age, and above all St. *Gregory Nazianzen*, who is called *the Divine* by excellence, of having altered, in this point, the Doctrine of the three foregoing Ages. But it will not appear very likely, that *M. Daille* should understand the Sentiments of the Fathers of the first three Ages, better than those who gathered, as I may say, the succession of their Doctrine after their Deaths; and this will be so much the less credible, because the Fathers of the fourth Age were so far from perceiving they introduced any Novelty in that Worship, that this Minister, on the contrary, has quoted several express Texts, by which he shows clearly, they pretended in Praying to Saints, to follow the example

of

*terminates in God alone.*

of their Predecessors. But without any further examination what might be the Sentiments of the Fathers of the three first Ages, I will content my self with what *M. Daille* is pleased to grant, allowing us so many great Men who taught the Church in the fourth Age. For tho' he has taken upon him, twelve hundred Years after their Deaths, to give them in derision the name of a kind of Sect, calling them *Reliquarists*, that is to say, Relique-honourers; yet I hope those of his Communion will have more respect for these great Men. They dare not at least accuse them of falling into Idolatry, by praying to Saints, or of destroying that trust which Christians ought to put in *JESUS CHRIST*: and it is to be hoped henceforwards they will not reproach these things to us, when they consider they cannot do it without accusing at the same time these excellent Men, whose Sanctity and Learning they profess a reverence for, as well as we. But seeing our design is here to expound our Belief, rather than to show who were the defenders of it, we must continue our explication.

## SECT. IV.

### Invocation of Saints.

THe Church in teaching it is profitable to pray to Saints, teaches us to pray to them in the same Spirit of Charity, and according to the same order of Fraternal Society, which moves us to demand assistance of our Brethren living upon Earth; and the Catechism of the Council of *Trent* concludes from this Doctrin, That if the quality of Mediator, which the Scripture gives to *JESUS CHRIST*, received any prejudice from the Intercession made to the Saints, who reign with God, it would receive no less from the Intercession made to the Faithful who live with us.

*Ca. Rom. part 3. tit. De Cultu & Invoc. Sanct.*

This Catechism shows us clearly the extreme difference betwixt our manner of imploring God's Assistance, and that of imploring the Aid of Saints: For (saith it) *we pray to God, either to give us good things, or to deliver us from evil; but because the*

*Part 4. tit. Quis orandus sit?*

*Invocation of Saints.*

the Saints are more acceptable to him than we are, we beg of them to undertake our cause, and to obtain for us those things we stand in need of. From whence it comes to pass, that we use two very different Forms of Prayer; for to God the proper manner of speaking is to say, HAVE PITY ON US, HEAR OUR PRAYER; whereas we only desire the Saints TO PRAY FOR US. From whence we ought to understand, that in what Terms soever, those Prayers, which we address to Saints, are couched, the intention of the Church, and of her Faithful, reduces them always to this form, as the Catechism presently after confirms.

*Ibid.*

But it is good to consider the Words of the Council it self, which prescribing to Bishops how they ought to speak of the Invocation of Saints, obliges them to teach, *That the Saints who reign with* JESUS CHRIST, *offer up to God their Prayers for Men. That it is good and profitable to invocate them after an humble manner, and to have recourse to their Prayers, Aid, and Assistance, to obtain of God his Benefits through our Lord* JESUS

*Seff.* 25. *Dec. de Invoc. &c.*

JESUS CHRIST *his Son, who is our sole Saviour and Redeemer*. After which the Council condemns those who teach a contrary Doctrine. We see then, to invocate the Saints, according to the sense of this Council, is to have recourse to their Prayers for obtaining Benefits from God through *JESUS CHRIST*. So that in reality we do not obtain those Benefits, which we receive by the intercession of the Saints, otherwise than through *JESUS CHRIST* and in his Name; seeing these Saints themselves pray in no other manner than through *JESUS CHRIST*, and are not heard but in his Name. This is the Faith of the Church, which the Council of *Trent* has clearly explicated in few words. After which we cannot imagine that any one should accuse us of forsaking *JESUS CHRIST*, when we beseech his Members, who are also ours, his Children, who are our Brethren, and his Saints, who are our first Fruits, to Pray with us, and for us to our common Master, in the name of our common Mediator.

The same Council explicates clearly

## Invocation of Saints.

clearly and in few words, what is the intention of the Church, when she offers up to God the dreadful Sacrifice to honour the memory of his Saints. This honour which we render them in Sacrificing, consists in naming them in the Prayers we offer up to God, as his faithful Servants; and in rendring him thanks for the Victories which they have gained, and in humbly beseeching him that he would vouchsafe to favour us by their intercession. St. *Augustin* has told us twelve hundred years ago, that we ought not to think any sacrifices were offered to the Holy Martyrs, altho' the practice of the universal Church in that time was to offer Sacrifice upon their holy Bodies, and at their *Memories*; that is to say, before those places where their pretious reliques were conserv'd. This Father has moreover added, *that they made a commemoration of the Martyrs at the Holy Altar, in the Celebration of the Sacrifice; not to pray for them as they do for other persons who are dead; but rather, that they might pray for us.* I relate the Sentiments of this Holy Bishop, because the Council of *Trent*

*8. de Civ.* *27.*

*Tract. 84. in Job.* *Serm. 17. in verb. Apost.*

*Conc. Trid. Sess. 22. c. 3.* makes use of his very words almost to teach the Faithful, that *the Church does not offer Sacrifice to the Saints, but to God alone, who has crowned them; that the Priest also does not address himself to St. Peter and St. Paul, saying,* I OFFER UP TO YOU THIS SACRIFICE; *but rendring thanks to God for their Victories, he demands their Assistance, to the end those whose Memory we celebrate upon Earth, would vouchsafe to pray for us in Heaven.* After this manner it is we honour the Saints, that we may obtain the Graces of God by their Intercession; and the Principal of those *Graces* we hope to obtain, is that of imitating them: to which we are excited by the consideration of their admirable Examples, and by the honour which we render in the Presence of *God* to their happy Memories.

Those who will rightly consider the Doctrine we have proposed, will be obliged to grant us, that as we do not rob *God* of any of those perfections peculiar to his infinite Essence: so we do not attribute to Creatures any

any of these qualities, or operations proper to God alone: which distinguisheth us so fully from Idolaters, that we cannot comprehend why such a Title should be given us.

And when these Gentlemen of the pretended Reformation object, that by addressing our Prayers to the Saints, and honouring them all the World over as present, we attribute to them a certain kind of Immensity, or at least the knowledg of the Secrets of Hearts, which God has nevertheless reserved to himself, as it appears by so many testimonies of Scripture; they do not sufficiently reflect upon our Doctrine. For, in fine, without examining what grounds may be had to attribute to the Saints some certain degree of knowledg as to those things which are acted amongst us, or also of our secret thoughts, it is manifest that to say a Creature may have the knowledg of these things, by a light communicated to him by God, is not to elevate a Creature above his condition. The Example of the Prophets justify this clearly, God having not disdained

disdained to discover future things to them, tho they appear much more particularly reserved to his own knowledge.

Moreover, never any Catholic yet thought the Saints knew our necessities by their own Power, no nor the desires which move us to address our secret Prayers to them. The Church contents herself to teach, with all Antiquity, these Prayers to be very profitable to such who make them, whether it be the Saints know them by the ministry and communication of Angels, who, according to the testimony of Scripture, know what passes amongst us, being established by Gods order, as administring Spirits, to cooperate with us in the work of our Salvation; whether it be that God himself makes known to them our desires by a particular *Revelation*; or lastly, whether it be that he discovers the secret to them in his *divine Essence* in which all truth is comprised. So that the Church has not decided any thing about these different methods, which God might be pleased to make use of for that end.

But let these means be what they will,

## Invocation of Saints. 77

will, it is always certain the Church does not attribute to the Creature any of the divine perfections, as the Idolaters did; seeing she permits us not to acknowledg, even in the greatest Saints, any degree of Excellency which does not proceed from God;nor any acceptableness in his Sight,but by their vertues; nor any vertue,which is not a gift of his Grace; nor any knowledge of human affairs, but what is communicated to them; nor any Power to assist us, but by their Prayers; nor,in fine, any felicity, but by a submission and a perfect conformity to his divine will.

It is therefore true, that by examining what are our interiour sentiments concerning the Saints,it will be found we do not raise them above the condition of Creatures; and from thence one ought to judge of what nature that exteriour honour is, which we render them;exteriour veneration: being established to testify the interiour sentiments of the Mind.

But because this honour,which the Church renders to the Saints,appears principally before their Images and
holy

holy Reliques, it will be proper to explicate her belief concerning them.

## SECT. V.
### Images and Reliques.

*Conc. Trid.*
*Sess. 24.*
*Dec. de In-*
*voc. &c.*

AS for Images, the Council of Trent forbids us expresly *to believe any divinity or vertue in them, for which they ought to be reverenced; to demand any favour of them, or to put any trust in them,* and ordains that all the honour which is given to them should be referred to the Saints themselves who are represented by them.

All these words of the Council are like so many characters to distinguish us from Idolaters, seeing we are so far from believing with them any Divinity annexed to the Images; that we do not attribute to them any other vertue but that of exciting in us the remembrance of those they represent.

The honour we render Images is grounded upon this. No Man, for example, can deny but that when we look upon the figure of *JESUS CHRIST* crucified, it excites in us a more lively remembrance of him, *who loved us so as to deliver himself*

*up*

*up to Death for us.* While this Image being present before our Eyes, causes so pretious a remembrance in our Souls, we are moved to testify by some exteriour signs how far our gratitude bears us; and by humbling our selves before the Image, we show what is our submission to our Saviour. So that to speak precisely, and according to the Ecclesiastical stile, when we honour the Image of an Apostle or a Martyr, our intention is not so much to *honour the Image, as to honour the Apostle or the Martyr in presence of the Image.* Thus the Roman Pontifical tells us, and the Council of Trent expresses the same thing, when it says, *that the Honour we render to Images, has such a reference to those they represent; that by the means of those Images which we Kiss, and before which we Kneel, we adore* JESUS CHRIST, *and honour the Saints, whose Types they are.*

*Gal. 2.*

*Pont. Com. de Bened. Imag. Sess. 25. Dec. de Inv. &c.*

In fine, one may know with what Intention the Church honours Images, by that honour which she renders to the Cross and to the Bible. All the World sees very well, that before the

1 Pet. 2. the Cross she adores him who *bore our Iniquites upon the wood*; and that if her children bow the head before the Bible, if they rise up out of respect when it is carried before them, and if they kiss it reverently, all this Honour is referred to the eternal Verity which it proposeth to us.

They must have but little Justice who treat with the term of *Idolatry* that *religious sentiment* which moves us to uncover our heads, and bow them before the Image of the Cross, in remembrance of him who was crucified for the love of us, and it would be too much blindness not to perceive the excessive difference betwixt those who put their trust in Idols, out of an opinion that some divinity, or some vertue was, as I may say, tied to them, and those who declare, as we do, that they will not make use of Images, but to raise their minds towards heaven, to the end they may there honour *JESUS CHRIST* or his Saints, and in the Saints God himself, who is the Author of all Sanctity & Grace.

After the same manner we ought to understand that Honour which we
pay

## Images and Reliques.

pay to Reliques, following the Example of the Primitive Church; and if our Adversaries would but consider that we look upon the Bodies of Saints, as having been Victims offered up to God either by Martyrdom or by Penance, they would not think the Honour which we pay them upon this account, could alienate us from that which we render to God himself.

We may say in general, That if they would but consider how the affections which we bear to any one propagates it self, without being divided, to his Children, to his friends, and after that, by several degrees, to the representation of him, to any remains of him, and to any thing which renews in us his remembrance; If they did but conceive that Honour has the like progression, seeing Honour is nothing else but Love mixed with Respect and Fear; in fine, If they would but consider, that all the exteriour Worship of the Catholic Church has its source in God himself, and returns back again to him: they would never believe

believe ; this Worship, which he himself alone animates, could excite his Jealousie. They would, on the contrary, see, that if God, as jealous as he is of the love of Men, does not look upon us as dividing our selves betwixt him and Creatures, when we love our Neighbour for the love of him; the same God, tho jealous of the Honour which his Faithful pay him, cannot look upon them as dividing that Worship which is due to him alone, when, out of respect to him, they honour those whom he has honoured.

It is true, nevertheless, that seeing the sensible marks of reverence are not all of them absolutely necessary, the Church might without the least alteration in her Doctrine, extend these exteriour Practices more or less, according to the different exigences of times, places, or occurrences, being desirous that her children should not be slavishly subject to sensible things, but only excited, and, as it were, advertised by their means to fly to God, and to offer up to him in Spirit and in Truth that rational service

vice which he expects from his creatures.

One may see by this doctrin with what truth I affirmed, that a great part of our Controversies would vanish by the sole understanding of the *Terms*, if these Points were but discussed with charity. And if our adversaries would but with moderation consider the foregoing Explications, which comprehend the express doctrin of the Council of *Trent*, they would cease to accuse us of injuring the Mediation of *JESUS CHRIST*, of invocating the Saints, and adoring Images after a manner which is peculiar to God alone. It is true, that seeing, in one sense, Adoration, Invocation, and the name of Mediator are only proper to God and *JESUS CHRIST*, it is no hard matter to misapply these terms, whereby to render our doctrine odious. But if they be strictly kept to that sense in which we use them, these objections and accusations will lose their force; and if any other less important difficulties remain to these *Gentlemen* of the Pretended Reform'd Religion, sincerity will

will oblige them to acknowledge they are satisfied as to the principal subject of their complaints.

Furthermore, there is nothing so unjust as to accuse the Church of placing all her Piety in these Devotions to the Saints, seeing, as we have already observed, the Council of *Trent* contents it self to teach the Faithful, that this Practice is *good and beneficial*, without saying any more of it. So that the intention of the Church is only to condemn those who reject this Practice, either out of disrespect or error. She is obliged to condemn them, because she is obliged not to suffer any Practice which is beneficial to Salvation to be despised, nor a Doctrine authorised by *Antiquity* to be condemned by *Novellists*.

*Sess. 25. Dec. de Inv. &c.*

## SECT. VI.
### *Justification.*

THe Doctrine of Justification will shew yet more clearly how many Difficulties may be ended by a plain Exposition of our Sentiments.

Those who are never so little versed in the History of the Pretended Re-

Reformation, are not ignorant how the first Authors propos'd this Article to all the World as the principal of all the rest, and as the most essential cause of their separation: So that this is the most necessary to be well understood.

We believe, in the first place, that *Our sins are freely forgiven us by the divine mercy, for JESUS CHRIST's sake.* These are the express terms of the Council of *Trent,* which adds, that *we are said to be justified* gratis, *because none of those acts which precede Justification, whether they be Faith or Good Works, can merit this Grace.*    *Conc. Trid. Sess.* 6. *c.* 9.

*Ibid. c.* 8.

Seing the Scripture explicates the *remission of sins,* by sometimes telling us that *God covers them,* and sometimes that *he takes them away, and blots them out by the Grace of his Holy Spirit, which makes us new creatures;* we believe, that, to form a perfect Idea of the Justification of a Sinner, we must joyn together both these Expressions. For which reason we believe our sins not only to be *covered,* but also *entirely washed away* by the Blood of *JESUS CHRIST,* and by the Grace of Regeneration;     *Tit.* 3. 5, 6, 7.

necessary duty of a Christian righteousness, which obliges us to confess humbly with St. *Augustine*, that our Justice in this life consists rather in the remission of Sin, than in the perfection of Vertues.

### SECT. VII.
#### Merits of Good Works.

AS to the Merit of Good works, the Catholic Church teacheth us, that *eternal life ought to be proposed to the Children of God, both as a Grace, which is mercifully promised to them by the Mediation of our Lord* JESUS CHRIST, *and as a recompence which is faithfully rendred to their good Works, and Merits, in vertue of this Promise.* These are the proper terms of the Council of *Trent*. But lest human Pride should flatter it self with an opinion of a presumptuous merit, the same council teacheth us, that all the price and value of a Christians works proceeds from the sanctifying Grace which is given us *gratis* in the Name of *JESUS CHRIST*, and that it is an effect of the

*Sess.* 6. 16.

*Ibid.*

*Merits of Good Works.*

the continual Influence of this Divine Head upon its Members.

Really the Precepts, Exhortations, Promises, Threatnings, and Reproaches of the *Gospel*, shew clearly enough, we must work out our Salvation by the co-operation of our Wills together with the Grace of God assisting us: But it is one of our First Principles, That the Free-will can act nothing conducing to Eternal Happiness, but as it is moved and elevated by the Holy Ghost.

So that the Church knowing it is this Divine Spirit which works in us by his Graces all the Good we do, she is obliged to believe the Good Works of the Faithful are very acceptable to God, and of great consideration before him: and it is just she should make use of the word *Merit*, with all Christian Antiquity, whereby she may principally denote the value, the price, and the dignity of those Works which we perform through Grace. But seeing all their Sanctity comes from God, who produces them in us, the same Church has in the Council of *Trent* received these words

## Merits of Good Works. 89

words of St. *Augustin*, as a Doctrine of Catholic Faith, That *God crowns his own Gifts in crowning the Merits of his Servants.*

We beg of those who love Truth and Peace, that they woud be pleased here to read the words of this Council a little more at length, to the end they may once for all disabuse themselves of those false impressions which have been given them concerning our Doctrine. *Although we see,* say the Fathers in this Council, *that holy Writ esteems Good Works so much, that JESUS CHRIST himself promises, That a glass of cold water given to the poor shall not want its reward; and that the Apostle testifies how a moment of light pain endured in this world, shall produce an eternal weight of Glory: nevertheless, God forbid a Christian should glory in himself, and not in our Lord, whose Bounty is so great to all men, that he will have those gifts which he bestows upon them to be their merits.*   *Sess. 6. c. 16.*

This Doctrine is dispersed throughout the whole *Council,* which teacheth us in another Session, That *we, who can do nothing of our selves, can do all*   *Sess. 14. c. 8.*
things

Will the Church never be able to perswade her Children, now become her Adversaries, neither by the Exposition of her Faith, nor by the Decisions of her Councils, nor by the Prayers in her Sacrifice, that her belief is, she can have no life but in *JESUS CHRIST*, and that she has no hope but in him? This hope is so firm, it makes the Children of God, who walk faithfully in his ways, find *a peace which surpasseth all understanding*, as the Apostle tells us. Phil. 4.7. But tho this hope be stronger than the promises and menaces of the World, and sufficient to calm the troubles of our Consciences; yet it does not wholly extinguish Fear: for tho we be assured God will never abandon us of his own accord, yet we are never certain we shall not lose him by our own fault, in rejecting his Inspirations. He has been pleased by his saving fear to mitigate that confidence which he has infused into his children, because, as St *Augustin* tells us, such is our Infirmity in this place of temptations and dangers, that an absolute security would produce tepidity

and

and pride in us, whereas this fear, which, according to the Apostles command, *makes us work out our Salvation with trembling*, renders us more vigilant, and makes us rely with a more humble dependence upon him, *who works in us by his Grace, both to will, and to do, according to his good Pleasure*, as the same St. Paul expresses it.

*Phil.* 2.12.

*Ibid.* 13.

Thus you have seen what is most necessary in the Doctrine of Justification; and our Adversaries would be very unreasonable, if they should not confess that this Doctrine suffices to teach Christians they are obliged to refer all the Glory of their Salvation to God through *JESUS CHRIST*.

If the Ministers after this should go about to move questions about subtilties, it is good to advertise them, that it becomes them not now to be so scrupulous in our behalfs, after having granted what they have done to the *Lutherans*, and their own Brethren, concerning Predestination and Grace. This their conduct towards them, ought to have taught them in this matter to reduce themselves to what

what is absolutely necessary for the establishment of the foundations of Christian Piety.

But if they could but once resolve to prefix these limits to themselves, they would be presently satisfied, and they would cease to accuse us of annulling the Grace of God, by attributing all to our good Works; seeing we have shown them in such clear terms of the Council of *Trent*, these three Points, so decisive as to this matter; *That our Sins are pardoned us out of pure Mercy, for the sake of* JESUS CHRIST.; *That we are indebted for that Justice which is in us by the Holy Ghost to a liberality* gratis *bestowed upon us; and that all the good works we do are but so many gifts of his Grace.*

And indeed we must acknowledg, that the learned of their Party do not contend so much of late about this Subject, as they did formerly, and there are but few who do not now confess, there ought not to have been a breach upon this Point. But if this important difficulty about Justification, upon which their first

Authors laid all their stress, be not looked upon now as essential by the wisest Persons amongst them, we leave them to think what they ought to judge of their Separation, and what hopes there would be of an Union, if they would but overcome their Prejudice, and quit the Spirit of Contention.

## SECT. VIII.

*Satisfactions, Purgatory, and Indulgences.*

WE must farther explicate after what manner we believe we can make Satisfaction to God through his Grace, to the end we may not leave any doubt upon this matter uncleared.

Catholics unanimously teach, that *JESUS CHRIST*, God and Man, was solely capable, through the infinite Dignity of his Person, to offer up to God a sufficient Satisfaction for our *Sins*. But having satisfied superabundantly, he could apply this infinite Satisfaction after two manners: either by an entire Remission, without reserving any punishment: or else by by changing a greater punishment into a less, that is, an eternal pain into a temporal. This first manner being more compleat, and more conformable to his Goodness, he makes use of it immediately in Baptism: but we believe he makes use of the second in the pardon he grants to those who fall after Baptism, being carried in some manner to it by the ingratitude of those who have abused his first Gifts; so as they are to suffer some temporal pain, tho the eternal be remitted.

It must not be hence concluded, that *JESUS CHRIST* has not fully satisfied for us; but, on the contrary, that having obtained an absolute Dominion over us, by the infinite Price he has given for our Salvation, he grants us pardon, upon what condition, what law, or with what restriction it pleases him.

We should be injurious and ungrateful to our Saviour, should we dare to deny the infinite Value of his Merits, under pretense that when he pardons us the Sin of *Adam*, he does not at the same time free us from all the consequences of it, but leaves us still subject to Death, and so many other corporeal and spiritual infirmities, which this Sin brought upon us. It suffices that *JESUS CHRIST* has once paid the price by which we shall be one day entirely freed from the evils which overwhelm us; it is our parts to embrace with humility and thanksgiving every part of his benefits, by considering by what progress it pleases him to procure our deliverance, according to that order which his Wisdom has established for our good, and for a more clear manifestation of his Bounty and Justice.

Upon the like account we ought not to think it strange, that he, who has shown us so great Mercy in Baptism, should be more severe towards us, after our having violated our holy promises. It is just, yes and beneficial to our Salvation, that God in remitting our Sin together with the eternal pain which we deserved for it, should exact of us some temporal Pain to retain us in our duties; lest if we should be too speedily freed from

the

the Bonds of Justice, we should abandon our selves to a temerarious Confidence, abusing the facility of a Pardon.

It is then to satisfie this Obligation, we are subjected to some painful Works, which we must accomplish in the Spirit of Humility and Penance; and it was the necessity of these satisfactory Works which obliged the Primitive Church to impose upon Penitents those Pains called Canonical.

When therefore she imposes upon Sinners painful and laborious works, and they undergo them with humility, this is called *Satisfaction*; and when, regarding the fervour of the Penitents, or some other Good Works which she has prescribed them, she pardons some part of that Pain which is due to them, this is call'd *Indulgence*.

The Council of *Trent* proposes nothing else to be believed concerning *Indulgences*, but that *the power to grant them has been given to the Church by* JESUS CHRIST, *and that the use of them is beneficial to Salvation*; to which this Council adds, *That this* *power* 

*Contin. Sess. 25. Dec. de Indulg.*

*Satisfactions, Purgatory,*

this Power ought to be retained, yet nevertheless used with moderation, lest Ecclesiastical discipline should be weakned by an over-great facility: which shows the manner of granting Indulgences to regard discipline.

Those who depart this Life in Grace and Charity, but nevertheless indebted to the divine Justice some Pains which it reserved, are to suffer them in the other Life. This is what obliged all the Primitive Christians to offer up Prayers, Alms-deeds and Sacrifices, for the Faithful who departed in Peace and in the Communion of the Church, with an assured Faith that they could be assisted by these means. This is what the Council of *Trent* proposes to our Belief, touching the Souls detained in Purgatory, without determining in what their pains consist, or many other such like things; concerning which this holy Council demands great moderation, blaming those who divulge what is uncertain or suspected.

Such is the innocent and holy Doctrine of the Catholic Church touching Satisfactions, which has been imputed

puted to her as so great a crime. If after this Explication, those of the Pretended Reform'd Religion accuse us of injuring the *Satisfaction* of *JESUS CHRIST*, they must have forgotten what we told them, that *our B. Saviour paid the full price of our Redemption; that nothing is wanting in this price, because it is infinite; and how these remaining pains, of which we have spoken, come not from any defect in the payment, but from a certain order which he has established to retain us in a saving discipline by just apprehensions.*

But if they also tell us, *we believe we can of our selves satisfie for some part of the pain due to our sins*; we can with confidence assure them, the contrary appears by the Maxims we have established; which Maxims make it clearly appear, that our Salvation is no other but a work of Mercy and Grace; that what we do by the Grace of God is no less his work, than what he does alone by his absolute Power; and lastly, that what we give to him, appertains no less to him, than what he gives to us. To which we must add, That what we call *Satisfaction*,

fol-

*Satisfactions, Purgatory,*

following the Example of the Primitive Church, is, after all, nothing but the application of the infinite *Satisfaction* of *JESUS CHRIST*.

This very Consideration ought to appease those who are offended when we tell them, That God is so well pleased with fraternal Charity, and the Communion of Saints, that he frequently also accepts of those Satisfactions which we offer up one for another. It seems these Men do not conceive how much all we are belongs to God, nor how all the Kindnesses which his Bounty makes him have for the Faithful, the Members of *JESUS CHRIST*, are necessarily referred to this Divine Head. But certainly those who have read and considered how God himself inspires his Servants with a desire to afflict themselves with Fasting, Hair-cloth, and Ashes, not only for their own Sins, but also for the Sins of all the People, will not be astonished if we say, that being touched with the delight he has to gratifie his Friends, he mercifully accepts of the humble Sacrifice of their voluntary

*and Indulgences.*

voluntary mortifications, in abatement of those chastisements he prepared for his people: which shows that being satisfied by these, he renders himself more mild towards the others, by this means honouring his Son *JESUS CHRIST* in the communion of his members, and in the holy society of his mystical body.

### SECT. IX.

*The Sacraments.*

THE Order of Doctrine requires we should now speak of the Sacraments, by which the merits of *JESUS CHRIST* are applyed to us. Seeing the disputes we have concerning them, if we except the Eucharist, are not so hot as the others; we will in the first place clear, in short, the cheifest difficuties which are raised concerning the other, and reserve the Eucharist, as the most important of all the rest, till the last.

The Sacraments of the new Covenant are not sacred signs only, which represent Grace; nor seals which confirm it; but the Instruments
of

of the Holy Ghoſt, which ſerve to apply it to us, and which confer it upon us by vertue of the words which are pronounced, and the exteriour action which is performed, upon condition we put not any Impediment by our not being rightly diſpoſed.

Whilſt God annexes ſo great Grace to exteriour ſigns, which have not of their own nature any proportion with ſo admirable an effect, he ſhows us clearly, that beſides all we can do interiourly of our ſelves by our good diſpoſitions, there muſt neceſſarily intervene, before we can be juſtified, a ſpecial operation of the Holy Ghoſt, and a peculiar application of the merit of our Saviour, which is exhibited to us by the Sacraments. So that this Doctrine cannot be rejected without injuring the merits of *JESUS CHRIST*, and the operation of his divine power in our regeneration.

We acknowledg ſeven ſacred Signs or Ceremonies eſtabliſhed by *JESUS CHRIST*, as the ordinary means for the Sanctification and perfection of the new man. Their divine inſtitution

institution appears in the holy Scripture, either by the express words of *JESUS CHRIST*, who established them, or by the Grace which, according to the same Scripture, is annexed to them, and necessarily shows a divine Institution.

### Baptism.

Seeing little Children cannot supply the want of Baptism by acts of Faith, Hope and Charity, nor by the vow to receive this Sacrament; we believe that, if they do not really receive it, they do not in any manner partake of the Grace of Redemption, and therefore dying in *Adam*, they have not any part in *JESUS CHRIST*.

It is good to observe here how the *Lutherans* believe with the Catholic Church the absolute necessity of Baptism, and are astonished with her, that such a truth should be denied, which never any one before *Calvin* durst openly call in question, it was so firmly rooted in the Minds of all the Faithful.

Nevertheless, the *Pretended Reform'd* are

are not apprehensive voluntarily to let their Children die like the Children of Infidels, without bearing any Mark of Christianity, and without receiving any Grace, if their Deaths should chance to prevent the day of their Assembly.

### Confirmation.

Act. 8. 15, 17.

The Imposition of Hands practised by the Holy Apostles, to confirm the Faithful against Persecutions, having its principal Effect in the interiour Descent of the Holy Ghost, and the infusion of his Gifts, it ought not to have been rejected by our Adversaries, under pretence the Holy Ghost descends now no more visibly upon us. Thus all Christian Churches since the Apostles times have religiously retained it, making use also of Holy Chrism, to shew the vertue of this Sacrament by a more expres representation of the interiour Unction of the Holy Ghost.

### Penance, and Sacramental Confession.

We believe that *JESUS CHRIST* has been pleased, those, who have sub-

submitted themselves to the Authority of the Church by Baptism, and who have since violated the Laws of the Gospel, should come and submit themselves to the Judgment of the same Church in the Tribunal of Penance, where she exercises the Power which is given her of remitting and retaining sins. *Matth. 18. 18. Joh. 20. 23*

The Terms of that Commission which is given to the Ministers of the Church to absolve from sin, are so general, they cannot without temerity be restrained to public sins; and seeing, when they pronounce that Absolution in the Name of *JESUS CHRIST*, they only follow the express Terms of this Commission, the Sentence is look'd upon as rendred by *JESUS CHRIST* himself, by whom they are established Judges. It is this invisible High Priest who interiourly absolves the Penitent, whilst the Priest exteriourly exercises the Function.

This Penitential Court of Judicature being so necessary a curb to Liberty, so plentiful a source of wise Admonitions, so sensible a Consolation for Souls afflicted for their Sins, when

when their absolution is not only declared in general terms, as it is practised by the Ministers, but when they are in reality absolved by the authority of *JESUS CHRIST*, after a particular examination, and knowledg of the Case: we cannot believe our adversaries can look upon so many benefits without regretting their loss, and without being somewhat ashamed of a Reformation which has cast off so saving and so holy a practise.

### *Extream Unction*.

The Holy Ghost having, according to the testimony of St. *James*, annexed an express promise of remission of sins, and comfort of the sick, to Extream Unction, nothing is wanting to make this sacred ceremony a true Sacrament. It is only to be remarked, that according to the Doctrine of the Council of *Trent*, the sick are more relieved in respect of the soul than of the body; and that as the spiritual profit is always the principal object of the new law, so it is that also which we ought absolutely

*1 Jac.* 14, 55.

*Sess.* 14. c. 2. de Sac. Extr. unc.

to expect from this holy unction, if we be rightly disposed for it; whereas the ease in sickness is only granted with a respect to our eternal salvation, according to the secret dispositions of divine Providence, and the different degrees of preparation and faith which is found in the Faithful.

### Marriage.

When we consider how JESUS CHRIST has given a new form to Marriage, reducing this holy society to two persons immutably and indissolubly united; and when we see this inseparable union, the sign of his eternal union with his Church: we shall not have any difficulty to comprehend that the marriage of the Faithful is accompanied by the Holy Ghost, and by Grace; and we shall praise the divine bounty for having been thus pleased to consecrate the origin of our birth.

*Math. 19. 5. Eph. 5. 32.*

### Orders.

The Imposition of Hands, which the Administrators of sacred things receive, being accompanied with so apparent a vertue of the Holy Ghost and so full an infusion of his Grace,

*1 Tim. 4.
2 Tim. 2.*

Grace, it ought to be placed amongst the number of the Sacraments. And indeed we must acknowledge our Adversaries do not absolutely exclude the Consecration of Ministers, but only exclude it from the number of the Sacraments which are *common to the whole Church.*

<small>Conf. de Foy, Art. 35.</small>

### SECT. X.

*Doctrine of the Church touching the Real Presence of the Body and Blood of* JESUS CHRIST *in the Eucharist, and the manner how the Church understands these Words,* This is my Body.

WE are come, you see, at last to the Question of the Eucharist, where it will be necessary to explicate our Doctrine more fully, however without exceeding too much the Bounds we have prescribed our selves.

The Real Presence of the Body and Blood of our Saviour is solidly established by the Words of the Institution, which we understand literally; and there is no more reason to ask

### *This is my Body.*

ask us, why we fix our selves to the proper and literal sense, than there is to ask a Traveller why he follows the high Road. It is their parts who have recourse to the figurative sense, and who take by-paths, to give a Reason for what they do. As for us, who find nothing in the words which *JESUS CHRIST* makes use of for the Institution of this Mystery obliging us to take them in a figurative sense, we think that a sufficient Reason to determine us to the literal. But we are yet more powerfully engaged, when we come to consider in this Mystery the Intention of the Son of God, which I will explicate after the plainest manner I am able, and that by Principles which I think our Adversaries themselves cannot deny.

I say then, These words of our Saviour, *Take eat, this is my body given for you*, shews us, that as the ancient Jews did not in Spirit only unite themselves to the Immolation of the Victim which was offered for them, but that in reality they eat the sacrificed Flesh, which was to them a mark

*Matth.* 16.
*Luc.* 22.

mark of their partaking of that oblation: So *JESUS CHRIST* becoming himself our Victim, would have us really eat of the flesh of his Sacrifice, to the end the actual communication of this adorable flesh might be a perpetual testimony to every one of us in particular, that it was for us he took it, and for us he immolated it.

*Levit.* 6. 30.

God had forbidden the Jews to eat of the sin-offering, to teach them that a true expiation of their crimes was not to be accomplished in the Law, nor by the blood of Beasts; all the people lay, as it were, under an interdiction by this prohibition, without being able to have any actual participation of the remission of Sins. By a contrary reason it was necessary the Body of our Blessed Saviour, the true Host immolated for sin, should be eaten by the Faithful, to show them, by this eating, that the remission of sin was accomplished in the new Testament.

*Levit.* 17. 11.

God also forbid the Children of *Israel* to eat Blood; and one of the reasons

*This is my Body.*

sons for this Prohibition was, because the Blood was given us for the Expiation of our Souls. But on the contrary, our Blessed Saviour gives us his Blood to drink, because *it is shed for the remission of Sins.*

Matb. 36. 18.

So that the eating of the Body and Blood of the Son of God is as real at the Holy Table, as the Grace, the expiation of Sins, and the participation of the Sacrifice of *JESUS CHRIST* is actual and real in the new Covenant.

Nevertheless, seeing he desired to exercise our Faith in this Mystery, and at the same time, to free us from the horror of eating flesh, and drinking Blood in their proper Species, it was convenient he should give us them cloathed under another Species. But if the Considerations have obliged him to make us partake of the flesh of our Victim after another manner than the *Jews*, he was not for that obliged to deprive us in the least of the reality of his Substance.

It appears then, that *JESUS CHRIST*, to accomplish the antient Figures, and

and to put us in actual Possession of the Victim offered for our Sins, that *JESUS CHRIST* had intention to give us really his Body and Blood. Which is so evident, that our Adversaries themselves would have us believe they are of the same opinion with us in this, perpetually repeating how they deny not the actual Presence, nor the real Participation of the Body and Blood in the Eucharist. This we will examine hereafter, where we think it necessary to represent their Sentiments, after we have finished the Explication of those of the Church. But in the mean time we will conclude, that if the plainness of our Saviours' words has forced them to acknowledg, his express Intention was to give us in reality his Flesh, when he said, *This is my Body*, they ought not to be astonished, if we cannot consent to understand these words only in Figure.

In reality, it appears that the Son of God, who was so careful to explain to his Apostles what he taught them under Parables and Figures, having said nothing here to explicate himself,

## This is my Body.   113

himself, lest these words in their natural Signification. I know these Gentlemen pretend the Nature of the thing explains it self sufficiently, because we see very well, say they, what he presents us is nothing but Bread and Wine; but this reason vanishes, when we consider, he who speaks has an Authority which over-rules the Senses, and a Power which has Dominion over universal Nature.

The Son of God has no more difficulty to render his Body present in the Eucharist, by saying, *This is my Body*, than to Cure a Woman of her Infirmity, by saying, *Woman thou art freed from thy Infirmity*; or to preserve the Life of a young Man, by saying to his Father, *Thy Son liveth*; or to forgive the Sins of a Man sick of the Palsy, by saying to him, *Thy sins are forgiven thee*.   *Luc.* 13. 12. *John* 4. 50. *Mat.* 9. 2.

So that we rest precisely upon his words, not troubling our selves how he will execute what he has said. He who does what he will, by speaking does what he pleases; and it was more easy for the Son of God to force the Laws of Nature to verify his

his word, than it is for us to accommodate our Understandings to these kind of violent Interpretations, which breaks the La.. of common Discourse.

These Laws of Discourse teach us, that a sign which represents a thing naturally, receives often the name of the thing represented, it being as it were its nature to bring the Idea of the thing into the Mind. The same also happens, tho with some restriction, to instituted Signs, when they are received, and Persons accustomed to to them. But that, in establishing a Sign, which has no relation to the thing, as for example, a Morsel of Bread to signify the Body of a Man, the name of the thing signified should be given to it without any Explication, and before any agreement, as *JESUS CHRIST* has done in his last Supper, is a thing unheard of, and of which we find no example in holy Writ, not to say in any Language. Neither do the Gentlemen of the Pretended Reform'd Religion so fix themselves to the figurative Sense, which they would give to these words

of

of *JESUS CHRIST*, but that at the same time they acknowledg, he had intention in pronouncing them to give us in reality his Body and Blood.

## SECT. XI.

*Explication of these Words,* Do this in remembrance of me.

AFter having proposed the Sentiments of the Church, touching these words, *This is is my Body*, we must explicate what she thinks of those others, which *JESUS CHRIST* added, *Do this in remembrance of me.* It is manifest, the intention of the Son of God is to oblige us by these words, to remember the Death which he has endured for our Salvation, and St. *Paul* concludes from these same words, that we *declare the Death of our Saviour* in this Mystery. But they must not perswade themselves, the remembrance of our Saviours Death, excludes the real Presence of his Body: on the contrary, if they consider what we have lately explicated, they will clearly understand this Commemoration to be grounded upon

*Luc.* 22. 19.
1 *Cor.* 11. 24.
2 *Cor.* 11. 26.

F the

the real Presence. For as the *Jews* in eating of the Peace-Offerings remembred they had been immolated for them; in the same manner in eating of the flesh of *JESUS CHRIST* our Victim, we ought to remember he died for us. This very flesh then, eaten by the Faithful, not only renews in us the memory of his immolation, but confirms also the reality of it to us. And we are so far from having reason to say, that this solemn Commemoration, which JESUS CHRIST ordains us to make, excludes the Presence of his Body, that on the contrary, we see this tender remembrance which he would have us to make at the Holy Table of him, as immolated for us, is grounded upon This; that this very flesh ought to be there taken really, seeing in effect it is not possible for us to forget it was for us he gave his Body in Sacrifice, when we see he daily gives us the same Victime to eat:

Must Christians, under pretence of celebrating in the Lords Supper, the memory of the Passion of our Saviour, deprive this Pious Commemoration

*Do this in remembrance of me.*

ration of what it has most efficacious and tender in it; ought they not to consider, that *Jesus Christ* does not command them only to remember him, but to remember Him in eating of his Flesh and Blood? Consider the connexion and the force of his words. He does not say simply, as those of the Pretended Reformation seem to understand him, That the Bread and Wine of the Eucharist should be to us a *Memorial* of his Body and Blood; but he advertises us, that in doing what he has prescrib'd, that is, in receiving his Body and Blood, we should remember him. What is there in reality more powerful to make us remember him? And if Children do so tenderly remember their Parents, and their Bounties towards them, when they approach the Tombs where their Bodies are interred; how ought our remembrance, and our love to be excited, when we possess under these sacred Vails, under this mystical Sepulchre, this living and Life-giving Flesh, and this Blood yet flowing with his Love, and full of Spirit and Grace? But if our

F 2     Adversaries

Adversaries continue to tell us, That he who commands us to remember him, does not give us his proper Substance, we must, in fine, desire them to agree amongst themselves. They profess, they deny not the real Communication of the proper substance of the Son of God in the Eucharist. If their words are serious, if their Doctrine be not an illusion, they must necessarily say with us, the remembrance does not exclude all kinds of Presence, but only that which strikes the Senses. Their Answer shall be ours, seeing that tho' we affirm *JESUS CHRIST* to be present, yet we acknowledg at the same time he is not present after a sensible manner.

And if it should be demanded, how it comes to pass, that believing as we do, the Senses to have nothing to do in this Mystery, we should not believe it sufficient that *JESUS CHRIST* should be present by Faith: it is easy to answer, and to clear this Equivocal Objection. It is one thing to say, the Son of God is present to us by Faith, and another thing to
say,

*Eucharist.*

say, we know by Faith that he is present. The first manner of speaking, Imports only a moral Presence; but the second signifies to us a very real one, because our Faith is most real; and this real Presence known by Faith, is sufficient to work all the forementioned Effects in the *Just Habac. 2. Man, who lives by Faith.* 4.

### SECT. XII.

*Exposition of the* Calvinists *Doctrine concerning the real Presence.*

BUT to remove all Equivocations which *Calvinists* make use of in this matter, and show at the same time, how near they have approached to us, it will be convenient to add here the Exposition of their Sentiments, tho I only undertook to explicate the Doctrine of the Church.

Their Doctrine has two parts; the one speaks of nothing but the Figure, and the other of nothing but the reality of the *Body* and *Blood*. We shall see each of these parts in order.

They tells us first, This great Mira=cle

cle of the real Presence, which we admit, is useless; that it is enough for our Salvation, *JESUS CHRIST* died for us; that his Sacrifice is sufficiently applied to us by Faith; and that this application is sufficiently certified to us by the Word of God. They add, That if this Word must be clothed with sensible Signs, it is enough to give simple Symbols, such as the Water of Baptism, without any necessity of fetching the Body and Blood of *JESUS CHRIST* from Heaven.

There seems to be nothing more easy than this manner of explicating the Sacrament of the Lords Supper. Nevertheless, our Adversaries themselves do not think it ought to suffice them. They know such kind of imaginations made the *Socinians* deny the great Miracle of the Incarnation. God might have saved us, say these Hereticks, without so much difficulty; he had nothing to do, but to pardon our faults, and might have instructed us sufficiently, as well in Faith, as in Manners, by the Preaching and Examples of a Man full of the Holy-Ghost, without any need of making him a God. But the
*Calvinists*

*Calvinists*, as well as we, see the weakness of this Argument, which appears first from its not appertaining to us to deny or affirm Mysteries, according as they appear to us useful or unprofitable to our Salvation. God alone knows the Secret; and it is our business to render them useful and saving to us, in believing them as he proposes them, and in receiving his Graces after the manner he bestows them upon us. Secondly, not to enter into the question, whether it was possible for God to save us by any other means than the Incarnation, and Death of his Son, and not to meddle with that unnecessary dispute, which the Pretended Reform'd Religion treats of so at length in the Schools, it suffices, we have learnt from the Scriptures, that the Son of God has been pleased to testifie his Love to us by incomprehensible Effects. This love has been the Cause of this so real an union, by which he was made Man. This Love moved him to immolate the *same Body* for us, as really as he united himself to it. All these designs are consecutive, and this Love maintains

maintains it self in all things with the same vigour. So that, when it shall please him to make each of his Children experience the goodness he has testified to all in general, by giving himself to them in particular, he will find out a method to accomplish his Desires, by no less efficacious means, than those by which he had already accomplished our Salvation. Upon which account we must not be hereafter astonished, if he give to each of us the proper *Substance* of of his Body and Blood. He does it that he may imprint in our Hearts, that it was for us he took them, and for us he offered them up in Sacrifice. That which preceded, makes all that follows credible to us; the order of his Mysteries dispose us to believe all this ; and his express word permits us not to doubt of it.

Our Adversaries saw very well, that simple figures and signs of his Body and Blood would not content Christians, who are accustomed to the Bounties of a God, who gives himself

to

to us so really. Wherefore they will not suffer us to accuse them of denying a real and substantial participation of *JESUS CHRIST* in their Supper. They affirm, as well as we, that he makes us there Partakers *of his proper Substance*; they tell us, that he *nourishes and quickens us with the substance of his Body and Blood*; and judging it would not be enough to shew us, by some sign, that we are partakers of his Sacrifice, they say expresly, that the *Body of our Saviour, which is given us in the last Supper, assures us of it*: words very remarkable, which we will examin by and by.

Cat. Dim. 53.
Conf. of Faith, art. 36.

Cat. Dim. 52.

Behold then the Body and Blood of *JESUS CHRIST* present in our Mysteries, by the acknowledgment of the *Calvinists*: for what is communicated *according to its proper substance*, must be really present. It is true, they explicate this Communication, by saying, it is in *Spirit*, and by *Faith*: but it is true also, they will have it Real. And because it is impossible to make it intelligible how a Body, that is communicated to us only

in

in Spirit, and by Faith, can be communicated to us really, and in its proper substance, therefore they have not been able to continue firm in the two parts of a Doctrine so contradictory, and they have been obliged to acknowledg two things which cannot be true, but by supposing what the Catholic Church teacheth.

The first is, That JESUS CHRIST is given to us in the Eucharist after a manner which neither agrees with that of Baptism, nor the Preaching of the Gospel, but is peculiar to this Mystery. We shall see by and by the Consequence of this Principle: but let us first see how it is granted us by those of the Pretended Reformation.

I will not here alledge the Authority of any particular Author, but the proper words of their Catechism, where it explicates what concerns the last Supper. It does not only tell us in express terms, that *JESUS CHRIST* is given us in the Supper, in reality, and according to his *proper Substance*, but that, *tho' he be truly communicated*

*Dim.* 53.

*of the real Presence.*

communicated to us, both by *Baptism*, and the *Gospel*, yet nevertheless, it is only in part, and not fully. From whence it follows, that he is given us in the Lords Supper fully, and not in part.

There is a vast difference betwixt receiving in part, and receiving fully. If then we receive *JESUS CHRIST* every where else in part, and it be only in the Lords Supper, we receive him fully; it follows by the consent of our Adversaries, that we must look out for a participation in the last Supper which is proper only to this Mystery, and which does not agree with Baptism and Preaching; but at the same time it follows also, that this participation is not annexed to Faith, because Faith being generally dispersed through all the Actions of a Christian, is found in Preaching and in Baptism, as well as in the Lords Supper: In reality, it is remarkable, that what desire soever the Pretended Reformers had to render Baptism and Preaching equal to the last Supper, because *JESUS CHRIST* is there truly communicated to us us, they durst never affirm in their Catechisms, that *JESUS CHRIST* is given us, in his proper Substance, by Baptism and Preaching, as they say he is given in the Eucharist. They saw then, they could not avoid attributing to the Eucharist a manner of possessing *JESUS CHRIST* peculiar only to this Sacrament; and that Faith, which is common to all the Actions of a Christian, could not be this particular manner. But this peculiar manner of possessing *JESUS CHRIST* in the last Supper ought also to be real, seeing it gives to the Faithful the proper substance of the Body and Blood of *JESUS CHRIST.* So that we must conclude, from what they grant us, there is in the Eucharist a real manner of receiving the Body and Blood of our Saviour, which is not performed by Faith; and this is what the Catholic Church teaches.

*Dim.* 52. The second thing granted by the Pretended Reformers, is taken out of that Article which immediately follows that which I have already cited out of their Catechism; which is,

That

*of the real Presence.*

*That the Body of our Lord* JESUS, *for as much as it was once offered up in Sacrifice to reconcile us to God, is now given to assure us, we have a part in that Reconciliation.*

If there be any Sense in these Words, if they be not an useless sound, and a vain amusement, we ought to understand by them, that *JESUS CHRIST* does not give us a Symbol only, but his proper Body, to assure us, we partake of his Sacrifice, and of the Reconciliation of Mankind. But if the reception of the Body of our Lord assures us of our participation of the Fruits of his Death; this participation of the Fruits must necessarily be distinguished from the reception of the Body, seeing one is the pledg of the other. From whence, to proceed, I say, If our adversaries are forced to distinguish in the last Supper the participation of the Body of our Blessed Saviour, from the participation of the fruits of his Grace in his Sacrifice, they must also necessarily make a distinction between the participation of this Divine Body, and all kinds of Spiritual participation

participation by Faith. This latter participation will never furnish them with two distinct Actions, by one of which they receive the Body of our Saviour, and by the other, the benefit of this Sacrifice; no man being able to conceive what difference there is betwixt partaking by Faith of the Body of our Saviour, and partaking by Faith of the Fruit of his Death. They must therefore acknowledg, that besides the Communion, by which we spiritually partake of the Body of our Saviour, and also of his Spirit, by receiving the fruit of his Death; there is also a Real Communion of the Body of the same Saviour, which is to us a certain Pledg of the others being assured to us, if we put no impediment to such a Grace by an evil Disposition. This is necessarily included in the Principles they admit, and they will never be able to explicate this Truth, with the least shadow of Solidity, if they return not to the Sentiments of the Church.

Who will not here admire the force of Truth? All the consequences which follow from the acknowledged

Principles

Principles of our Adversaries, are perfectly understood in the sentiment of the Church-Catholics; the meanliest instructed, without difficulty conceive, that in the Eucharist there is a Communion with *JESUS CHRIST*, which is not to be found any where else. It is no difficulty for them to understand his Body *is given us, to assure us we partake of his Sacrifice and of his Death* They distinguish clearly betwixt these two necessary manners of uniting our selves to *JESUS CHRIST*; the one, in receiving his proper Flesh; the other, in receiving his Spirit: the first of which is granted us, as a certain Pledge of the second. But seeing these things are inexplicable in the sentiments of our Adversaries, tho on the other hand they cannot deny them, we must necessarily conclude, that Errour has thrown them into a manifest Contradiction.

I have been often astonished they did not explicate their Doctrine after a more plain manner. Why did they not always, without so many Formalities, persevere to say, that *JE-*

*JESUS CHRIST* having shed his Blood for us, represented to us this effusion, by giving us two distinct signs of his Body and Blood; that he was pleased indeed to give to these signs the name of the thing it self: that these sacred signs were pledges to assure us of our partaking of the fruit of his Death, and that we were spiritually nourished by the vertue of his Body and Blood? After so many endeavours to prove that signs often receive the names of the things signified, and that for this reason the sign of the Body might be called the Body, all this connection of Doctrine obliges them naturally to fix there. To render these signs efficacious, it sufficed the Grace of Redemption was annexed to them, or rather, according to their Principles, that it was in them confirmed to us. They needed not have tormented themselves, as they have done, to make us understand we receive the proper Body of our Saviour, to assure us we partake of the Grace of his Death. They were well enough satisfied to have the water of Baptism a sign of the Blood which

*of the real Presence.*

which washeth us; and it never entred into their fancies to say, we there received the proper substance of the Blood of our Blessed Saviour, to assure us his vertue is there diffused upon us. If they had argued after the same manner as to the Eucharist, their Doctrine would have been less embroyled. But those who invent and innovate, cannot express all they have a mind to. They find certain truths, and maxims established which incommode them, and force a violence upon their imaginations. The *Arians* would gladly have refused our Blessed Saviour the name of God, or the only Son of God. The *Nestorians* did not admit, but with reluctance, that kind of I know not what unity of person in *JESUS CHRIST*, which we find in their writings. The *Pelagians*, who denied Original sin, would also willingly have denied that Baptism was given to little children for the remission of sins: for by that means they would have been freed from the argument which Catholics drew from this practice to prove that Original defect:

But,

But, as I just now said, those who find some truths firmly established, have not the boldness, or rather impudence to overthrow all. Let the *Calvinists* ingenuously confess the truth; they would have been well pleased to acknowledg in the Eucharist the Body of our Blessed Saviour only figuratively, and the sole participation of his Spirit in effect, laying aside those great words of *Participation of his proper substance*, and the many others which import a real presence, and serve only to perplex them. It would have been more to their humour, to have acknowledged, in the Lords Supper, no other communion with *JESUS CHRIST*, but what is also common to Preaching and to Baptism, without telling us, as they have done, that in the Lords Supper *he is received in plenitude*, and every where else only *in part*. But however this was their Inclination, yet the very force of the terms oppose them, our blessed Saviour having said so precisely of the Eucharist, *This is my Body, This is my Blood*; which he never did of any other thing, nor upon any

any other occasion; what likelihood was there of rendring that common to all the Actions of a Christian, which his express word had annexed to one particular *Sacrament* ? And farther, the whole order of divine providence, the connexion of Doctrin and Holy Mysteries, the intention of *JESUS CHRIST* in his last Supper, the words themselves which he uttered, and the impression which they naturally form in the minds of the Faithful, give us nothing but the Ideas of his real presence. Therefore it was necessary our adversaries should find out some expressions, the sound of which might, at least, give us a confused Idea of this reality. When a man fixes himself either entirely upon Faith, as Catholics do; or entirely upon human Reason, as Infidels do, it is easie for him to establish a connected and uniform model of Doctrin. But when a man goes about to make a composition of one and the other, he always says somthing which he would not say, and afterwards falls into opinions, the sole contrarieties of which shew the manifest falsity of them.

This

This is what has hapned to these *Gentlemen* of the *Pretended Reform'd Religion*; and God has so permitted it, to facilitate their return to *Catholic Unity*. For, whereas their proper experience shews them, they must necessarily *express themselves as we do*, to *speak the Language of Truth*; ought they not to judge it necessary to *think as we do, to understand it right?* If they observe in *their own Belief* many expressions which have no sense but according to *our Tenets*, is it not sufficient to convince them, that *Truth* is not in its *full perfection but amongst us?* And ought not those *unconnected parts of Catholic Doctrine*, which are scattered here and there in their *Catechisms*, but which, as I may say, require to be united to the whole; ought they not, I say, to excite them to search, in the *Communion of the Church, a full and entire explication of the Mystery of the Eucharist?* They would, no doubt, be brought to it, did not *humane reflections* trouble & perplex their *Faith*, wch has too much dependence upon *sense*. But having shewn what *fruit* they ought to reap from the *Exposition of their Doctrine*,

let

let us finish the *Explicatio of our own.*

## SECT. XIII.

*Of Transubstantiation and Adoration, and in what sense the Eucharist is said to be a Sign.*

IT having been convenient, as was said before, that the Senses should not perceive any thing in this Mystery of Faith, it was necessary nothing should be changed, in respect of them, in the Bread and Wine of the Eucharist. Upon which account, being we see the same Species, and feel the same Effects as before in this Sacrament, we must not wonder, if the same name be given to them sometimes, and in some certain sense. Yet notwithstanding, Faith being attentive to His word, who performs what pleases him in Heaven and on Earth, acknowledges here no other Substance, but what is designed by the same word, that is to say, the proper Body and Blood of *Jesus Christ*, into which the Bread and Wine are changed; this is what we call *Transubstantiation.*

However, that real Verity which is interiourly contained in the Eucharist,

charist, hinders not the exterior and sensible part from being a sign; but a sign of such a Nature, that it is so far from excluding the reality of the thing signifyed, it bears it necessarily along with it, seeing that in effect, these words, *This is my Body*, pronounc'd upon that matter, which JESUS CHRIST himself made choice of, is to us a certain sign that his Body is present, and tho the Symbols appear always the same to our Senses, yet our Mind judges otherwise of them, and not according to Sense, because a superior Authority interposes. So that, whereas certain Species, and a certain sequel of natural impressions on our senses, have been accustomed to design to us the substance of Bread and Wine, the Authority of Him, in whom we believe, causes these same species to begin to shew us another substance. For we give ear to him who said, that *this, which we receive and eat, is his Body*; and such is the force of these words, as they hinder us from referring those exteriour appearances to the substance of Bread, and induce us to refer

fer them to the Body of JESUS CHRIST there present: Insomuch that the presence of such an adorable Object being rendered certain to us by this sign, we are not afraid to pay it our adorations.

I will not dwell upon the point of Adoration, because the most learned and most intelligent of our Adversaries have long since granted us, those who are perswaded of the real presence of *JESUS CHRIST* in the Eucharist ought to pay him in it their Adorations.

In fine, being once convinced, the all-powerful words of the Son of God operate whatever they declare, we believe that in the last Supper, they had their effect as soon as they were pronounced by him; and by a necessary Consequence we acknowledg the real Presence of his Body, before our receiving of it.

## SECT. XIV.
### Sacrifice of the Mass.

THese things being supposed, there remains no particular difficulty about the Sacrifice which we acknowledg in the Eucharist. We

We have observed two actions in this Mystery, which cease not to be distinct, tho one of them has a Relation to the other. The first is the consecration, by which the Bread and Wine are changed into the Body and Blood; and the second is the receiving, by which we partake of them.

In the Consecration, the Body and the Blood are mystically separated, because JESUS CHRIST said separately, *This is my Body*, *this is my Blood*; which includes a lively and efficacious Representation of the violent Death he suffered.

So that the Son of God is placed upon the Holy Table, in vertue of these words, cloathed with those signs which represent his Death, this is effected by Consecration; and this Religious action carries with it an acknowledgment of Gods soveraignty, in as much as JESUS CHRIST there present, renews and perpetuates, in some sort, the remembrance of his being obedient, even to the death of the Cross: So that there is nothing wanting to render this a true sacrifice.                    We

## Sacrifice of the Mass.

We cannot doubt but this Action, as distinct from that of Communicating, is of it self acceptable to God, and makes him look upon us with a more propitious Eye, because it represents to him that voluntary Death which his beloved Son has suffered for us Sinners, or rather places before his Eyes that very Son of his, under the signs of this Death, by which his Wrath had been appeased.

All Christians will confess the sole Presence of *JESUS CHRIST* to be a most Powerful Intercession before God for all mankind; according to the saying of the Apostle, That *JESUS CHRIST presents himself and appears for us before the Face of God.* So that we believe *JESUS CHRIST* being present upon the Holy Table, under this Figure of Death, intercedes for us, and represents continually to his Father that death which he has suffered for his Church.

It is in this Sense we say, *JESUS CHRIST* offers up himself to God for us in the Eucharist; it is after this manner we conceive this Oblation renders God more propitious to us,

*Heb.* 5.24.

G   and

and therefore we call this a Propitiatory Sacrifice.

When we consider what it is, *JESUS CHRIST* operates in this Mystery, and when we see him by Faith present upon this Holy Table, together with these Signs of death, we unite our selves to him in this Estate; we present him to God, as our only Victim, and our sole Propitiator by his Blood, confessing we have nothing to offer up to God but *JESUS CHRIST*, and the infinite Merit of his Death. We consecrate all our Prayers by this Holy Oblation, and in presenting *JESUS CHRIST*, to God we learn at the same time, to offer up our selves to the Divine Majesty in him, and by him, as living Sacrifices.

This is the Sacrifice of Christians, infinitely different from what was offered up in the Old Law: a Spiritual Sacrifice becoming the New Covenant, in which the presence of the Victim is only perceived by Faith; in which the Word of God is the Spiritual Sword which makes a Mystical separation betwixt the Body and the Blood; in which by consequence the

the Blood is only shed Mystically, and in which Death only intervenes by representation: and yet however a most real Sacrifice, in as much as *JESUS CHRIST* is there truly contained, and presented to his Father, under this Figure of Death: But a Commemorative Sacrifice, which is so far from taking away our adhesion to the Sacrifice of the Cross (as it is objected to us) on the contrary, it fixes us the firmer to it by all its circumstances; seeing it has not only an entire relation to it, but in reality, has neither being nor subsistence but by this relation, from whence it deriveth all the Vertue contained in it.

This is the express Doctrine of the Catholic Church in the Council of *Trent*, which teaches, that this Sacrifice is instituted only *to represent that which was once accomplished upon the Cross; to perpetuate the memory of it to the end of the World; and to apply to us the saving Vertue of it for the remission of those sins which we commit every day.* So that the Church is so far from believing, that

*Sess.* 22. *c.* 1.

something

something wants to perfect the Sacrifice of the Cross; on the contrary, she thinks it so perfect, and so fully sufficient, as what is added, is only instituted to celebrate the memory, and apply its Vertue.

By which the same Church acknowledges, that all the merit of the Redemption of Mankind depends upon the Death of the Son of God; and it ought to be understood, from all we have already expounded, that when we say to God in the Celebration of the Divine Mystery, *We offer unto you this Holy Host*, we pretend not by this Oblation, to make, or present to God a new payment of the price of our Salvation, but to offer up to him in our behalfs, the Merits of our Blessed *JESUS* there present, and the infinite price which he once paid for us upon the Cross.

The Gentlemen of the Pretended Reform'd Religion do not think they offend *JESUS CHRIST*, by offering him to God as present to their Faith; and if they believed him to be really there, what repugnance could they have to offer him up as truly

truly present; So that the whole dispute ought indeed to be reduced to the real presence alone.

From hence forwards, all those false Ideas, which these Gentlemen of the Pretended Reform'd Religion form to themselves of the Sacrifice which we offer, ought to be effaced. They ought freely to acknowledge Catholics pretend not to make a new propitiation to appease God a fresh, as if he had not been sufficiently satisfied by the Sacrifice of the Cross; or to make some addition to the Price of our Salvation, as if it were imperfect. All these things have no place in our Doctrine; because all that is here done, is intended by way of Intercession and Application, after the manner which we have now explicated.

## SECT. XV.
*The Epistle to the* Hebrews.

AFter this Explication, those mighty Objections drawn from the Epistle to the *Hebrews*, and so much enforced against us, will appear to have little reason in them: and it is in vain our Adversaries strive to prove,

prove, from the sentiments of the Apostle, that we annul the Sacrifice of the Cross. But because the best way to prove that two Doctrines are not opposite to one another, is to shew, by explicating them, that no propositions of the one is contrary to the propositions of the other; I think I am bound in this place to propose in short the Doctrine of this Epistle.

The Apostle intends in this Epistle to teach us, that a sinner could not avoid Death, but by substituting some one in his place to die for him; that whilst Men substituted only Beasts to be killed in their places, their Sacrifices operated nothing, but a publick acknowledgment of their having deserved Death; and that, seeing the Divine Justice could not be satisfied by so unequal an exchange, they begun again every day to slay new Victims; which was a certain mark of the insufficiency of that substitution: But that, since *JESUS CHRIST* had vouchsafed to die for Sinners, God being satisfied, by a Person so condignly sufficient substituting

ting of himself, nothing more to exact for the price of our Redemption. From whence the Apostle concludes, we ought not only to offer up no more Victims after *JESUS CHRIST*, but that *JESUS CHRIST* himself ought to be but once offered up to Death for us.

Let the Reader then, who is solicitous for his Souls Salvation, and a lover of Truth, reflect a little upon what we have said concerning the manner how *JESUS CHRIST* offers up himself to God for us in the Eucharist; I am certain, he will not find any Proposition contrary to those I have here related from the Apostle; or which weakens his Argument; so that nothing can be objected to us, but his silence upon this point. But those who would but consider the wise distribution which God makes of his secrets in the several Books of Scripture, would not oblige us to receive, from the sole Epistle to the *Hebrews*, all our instructions concerning a matter which was not necessary to the Subject of that Epistle; seeing the Apostle intends to explicate in it, it, the perfection of the Sacrifice of the Cross, and not the different manners which God has instituted to apply it to us.

And to remove all equivocation, if we take the word *Offer* in the sence it is made use of in this Epistle, as implying the actual Death of the Victim, we will publickly confess, that *JESUS CHRIST* is now no more offered up, neither in the Eucharist, nor any where else. But because this word has a larger signification in other places of Scripture, where it is often said, We offer up to God what we present before him; the Church, which forms her Language, and her Doctrine not from the sole Epistle to the *Hebrews*, but from the whole Body of the Holy Scripture, is not afraid to say, that *JESUS CHRIST* offers up himself to God wherever he appears before his Face upon our behalf, and that by consequence, he offers up himself in the Eucharist, according to the Holy Fathers expressions.

Now to imagine this manner, of *JESUS CHRIST*'s, presenting himself

*The Epistle to the* Hebrews. 147

himself to God, should injure the Sacrifice of the Cross, is what cannot in any kind be supposed without overthrowing the whole Scripture, and particularly this Epistle, which is so vehemently objected against us. For it must, by the same reason, be concluded, that when *JESUS CHRIST* offered up himself to God, *In entring into the World*, to substi- *Heb.* 10. 5. tute himself in place of those Victims, *which could not please him*, he injured *Heb.* 9. 24. that Action by which he offered up himself upon the Cross, that when he *continues to appear before God for us*, *Heb.* 9. 26. he weakens that Oblation, *by which he appeared once, by the immolation of* *Heb.* 7. 25. *himself*; and that *not ceasing to intercede for us*, he accuses of insufficiency that intercession which he made in dying with *so many tears*, *Heb.* 5. 7. *and such an exclamation.*

All this would be ridiculous. We must therefore understand, that *JESUS CHRIST*, who once offered up himself to be the humble Victim of the Divine Justice, does not cease to offer up himself always for

G 5 us;

us; that the infinite perfection of the Sacrifice of the Cross consists in this, that whatsoever preceded it, as well as what follows it, has an entire reference to it; that as what preceded it, was a preparation to it; so that which follows it, is the consummation and application of it; that in reality the payment of the price of our Redemption is no more reiterated, because it was fully discharged the first time; but that what applys that Redemption to us continues without ceasing; lastly, that we must make a distinction betwixt the things which are reiterated as imperfect, and those which are continued as perfect and necessary.

## SECT. XVI.

*Reflections upon the preceding Doctrin.*

WE conjure all those of the Pretended Reformation, to make some little Reflection upon what has been said concerning the Eucharist.

The Doctrin of the Real Presence has been the necessary foundation of it.

it. This Foundation is impugned by the *Calvinists*. There is nothing appears more important than this in our Controversies, seeing the Question is concerning the real Presence of *JESUS CHRIST* himself. There is nothing our Adversaries find more difficult to believe. And there is nothing in which we are so directly opposite, as in this.

In most other Disputes, when these Gentlemen hear us with calmness, they find the difficulties vanish, and that they are more offended with words, than with the things themselves. On the contrary, upon this subject, we agree more about the manner of speaking; because both sides use the words of *Real Participation*, and the like: But the fuller we explicate our selves, the more we find our selves opposed; because our Adversaries do not receive all the consequences of those truths which they admit, being discouraged (as I said) by the difficulties which Sence and Human Reason find in these *consequences*.

This is therefore, to say truly, the most difficult of our Controversies,

troversies, and that in which we are
most opposite to one another.

Nevertheless God has permitted
the *Lutherans* should adhere to the
belief of the real Presence as well as
we: and he has also permitted the
*Calvinists* should declare this Doctrine to have no poison in it; that it
does not subvert the foundations of
Salvation and Faith; and that it
ought not to break communion betwixt Brethren.

Let those of the *Pretended Reform'd
Religion*, who think seriously of their
Salvation, render themselves here attentive to that Order, which the divine Providence makes use of to bring
them insensibly nearer to us and
Truth. One may either intirely dissipate all the other grounds of their
complaints, or at least reduce them to
very few Heads, with a little explication. In this where we cannot hope to
conquer by this Method, they have
themselves removed the chief difficulty, by declaring this Doctrine to
*contain nothing in it contrary to Salvation, or to the fundamentals of Religion.*

It is true, the *Lutherans*, tho' they con-
cur

cur with us in the ground of the reality, yet admit not all the consequences of it. They put Bread together with the Body of *JESUS CHRIST*; some of them reject the Adoration; and they seem to acknowledge the Real Presence only in the Act of Receiving. But all the subtilty of the Ministers can never persuade ingenuous and understanding Persons, but that, if they maintain the Real Presence, which is the most important and the most difficult Point, they ought also to maintain the rest.

Moreover, the same Providence, which labours secretly for our nearer Union, and lays the Foundations of Reconciliation and of Peace in the midst of Bitterness and Disputes, has farther permitted the *Calvinists* to allow, that supposing these words, *This is my Body*, ought to be taken in a literal sense, *Catholics* reason better and more consequently than the *Lutherans*.

If I relate not the Passages which have been so often cited on this account, I hope I shall easily be excused, because all those, who are not obstinate,

obstinate, will grant us without difficulty, that the real Presence being supposed, our Doctrin is that which most naturally follows.

It is then an established Truth, that our Doctrin in this point contains nothing but the real Presence rightly understood. But we must not stop there; and we beseech the Pretended Reform'd to consider, we make use of no other things to explicate the Sacrifice of the Eucharist, but only such as are necessarily included in this reality of Presence.

If it should be asked us after this, how it comes then to pass the *Lutherans*, who believe the real Presence, should nevertheless reject the Sacrifice, which is according to us, only a consequence of it: our answer is in one word, that this Doctrine must be numbred amongst the other consequences of the real Presence, which these *Lutherans* have not understood, and which we have penetrated much better than they, as the *Calvinists* themselves confess.

If our Explications persuade these last, that our Doctrine about the Sacrifice

crifice is included in that of the real presence, they ought to see clearly that this mighty dispute of the Sacrifice of the Mass, which has filled so many Volumes, and occasioned so many Invectives, ought from henceforwards to be retrenched from the body of their controversies, because this point has not now any particular difficulty, and (which is much more important) because this Sacrifice, against which they have so great repugnance, is no other but a necessary consequence and a natural explication of a Doctrine, which, according to them, *has no venim in it*. Let them now examin themselves, and after this, try before God whether they have so much reason, as they imagine, to withdraw themselves from those Altars, where their fore-fathers received the Bread of life.

## SECT. XVII.

*Communion under both kinds.*

THere remains one other Consequence of this Doctrine to be examined, which is, that *JESUS CHRIST*

*CHRIST* being really present in the Sacrament, the Grace and Benediction is not annexed to the sensible Species, but to the proper substance of his Flesh, which is living, and lifegiving, because of the Divinity which is united to it. Upon which account, all those who believe the Real Presence, ought not to have any difficulty to communicate under one sole Species, because they there receive all that is essential to this Sacrament, together with a plenitude so secure, because there being now no real separation betwixt the Body and the Blood, (as hath been said) we receive entirely, and without division him, who is solely capable to satiate us.

This is the solid foundation, upon which the Church, interpreting the precept of Communion as declared, we may receive the Sanctification, which this Sacrament carries with it, under one sole species; and if she have reduced her Children to this sole species, it was not out of disesteem of the other, seeing, on the contrary, she did it to hinder those Irreverences, which the confusion and negligence
of

of people had occasioned in these later ages, reserving to her self, the re-establishment of communion under both kinds, according as it should become more advantagious to Peace and Unity.

Catholic Divines have made it appear to those of the pretended Reformation, how they themselves have made use of several such like Interpretations, in what belongs to the use of the Sacrament; but above all they had reason to remark this which is taken out of the 12 *chap.* of their discipline, Title of the Lords Supper, *art.* 7. where we find these words: *The Bread of the Lords Supper ought to be administred to those who cannot drink wine, upon their making protestation, that it is not out of contempt, and endeavouring what they can possibly, to obviate all Scandal even by approaching the cup as neer their mouths as they are able.* They have judged, by this regulation that both species were not, by the institution of *JESUS CHRIST*, essential to the Communion: otherwise they ought to have absolutely refused the Sacrament

ment to those, who could not receive it whole and entire, and not to give it them after a manner contrary to that which *JESUS CHRIST* had commanded; in which case their disability would have been their excuse. But our Adversaries conceived it would be an excessive rigour, not to allow at least one of the species to those, who could not receive the other; and as this condescendence has no ground in Scripture, they must acknowledge with us, the words, by which *JESUS CHRIST* proposes to us the two species, are liable to some interpretation, and that this interpretation ought to be declared by the authority of the Church.

But it might seem as if this article of their discipline, which was made in the Synod of *Poitiers* held in the year 1560, had been reformed by the Synod of *Verteüil* held in the year 1567. where it is said *the company is not of opinion, the bread should be administred to those who would not receive the Cup*. These two Synods nevertheless are no ways opposite. That of *Verteüil* speaks only of those

*who*

who will not receive the *Cup*; And that of *Poitiers* of those only *who cannot*. In effect, notwithstanding the Synod of *Vertueil*, this Article remains in their discipline, and has been also approved by a latter Synod than that of *Vertueil*, by the Synod of *la Rochell* in 1571, where this article was review'd, and put into that state in which it now is.

But supposing the Synods of the pretended Reform'd Religion had differed in their sentiments, it would only follow that the matter in question regards not Faith, and that it is of the number of those, which are at the Churches disposal according to their own Principles.

## SECT. XVIII.
*The written and unwritten Word.*

THERE remains nothing more now, but to explicate what Catholics believe touching the Word of God, and the Authority of the Church.

*JESUS CHRIST* having laid the Foundation of his Church by Preaching, the unwritten Word was the first Rule of Christianity; and when the Writings of the *New Testament* were added, this unwritten Word did not upon that account lose its Authority: which makes us receive with equal veneration all that was ever taught by the Apostles, whether by Writing, or by word of Mouth, as St. *Paul* himself has expresly declared. And it is a most certain sign, a Doctrine comes from the Apostles, when it is universally embraced by all Christian Churches, without any possibility of shewing its beginning. We cannot chuse but receive all that is established after this manner, with the submission due to Divine Authority; and we are perswaded those of the Pretended Reformation, who are not obstinate, are in the bottom of their Hearts of the same Opinion; it being impossible to believe a Doctrine, received from the beginning of the Church, can flow from any other source than that of the Apostles. Wherefore our Adversaries ought not to wonder if we, who are careful to gather together all our Fathers have

2 *Thess.* 2. 14.

have left us, should conserve the *Depositum* of Tradition as well as that of the Scriptures.

## SECT. XIX.
### The Authority of the Church.

THe Church being established by God to be the Guardian of Scripture and Tradition, we receive the Canonical Scriptures from her; and let our Adversaries say what they will, we doubt not but it is her Authority which principally determines them to reverence as Divine Books, the *Canticle of Canticles*, which has so few visible marks of a Prophetical Inspiration; the Epistle of St. *James*, which *Luther* rejected; and that of St. *Jude*, which might appear suspected because of some Apocryphal Books cited in it. In fine, it can only be from this Authority they receive the whole Body of Scripture, which all Christians accept as Divine, before their reading of it has made them sensible of the Spirit of God in it.

Being then inseparably bound, as we are, to the Holy Authority
of

of the Church, by means of the Scriptures which we receive from her Hands, we learn Tradition also from her; and by the means of Tradition we learn the true sense of Scripture. Upon which account the Church professes; she tells us nothing from her self, and that she invents nothing new in her Doctrine: she does nothing but declare the Divine Revelation, by the interiour Direction of the Holy Ghost, who is given to her as her Teacher.

That Dispute, which was raised in the very time of the Apostles, upon account of the Ceremonies of the Law, shews clearly, that the Holy Ghost explicates himself by the Church; and their Acts have by the Method by which that first Contest was decided, taught all succeeding Ages, by what Authority all other Differences are to be ended. So that as often as there shall happen any Disputes to cause a Division amongst the Faithful, the Church will interpose her Authority, and her Pastors assembled will say after the Apostles, *Act. 15.21.* *It has seemed good to the Holy Ghost,*
*and*

*and to us.* And when she has spoken, her Children will be taught, they ought not to begin again to examin those Articles once so resolved on; but are bound humbly to receive her Decisions. In this we shall follow the example of St. *Paul* and *Silas*, who carried this first Sentence of the Apostles to the Faithful, and were so far from permitting a new Discussion of what had been decided, that, on the contrary, *They went from place to place, teaching them to observe the Ordinances of the Apostles.* Acts 16. 4.

Thus it is the Children of God acquiesce in the Judgment of the *Church*, believing that from her Mouth they hear the Oracle of the Holy Ghost; and upon account of this belief it is, that after having said in our Creed, *I believe in the Holy Ghost*, we add immediately, *The Holy Catholic Church*; by which we oblige our selves to acknowledge an infallible and perpetual Verity in the Universal Church, because this very Church which we believe existent in all Ages, would cease to be the Church, if she ceased to teach the truth revealed

by

Moreover, if our Adversaries consult their Consciences, they will find the Name of the Church has more Authority over them, than they dare avouch in their Disputes: and I do not think there is any one prudent Man amongst them, who finding himself the only Person of a Perswasion, tho it appeared to him never so evident, but would abhor that Singularity; so true it is, that Men have need in these Matters to be supported in their Tenets, by the Authority of some Society that is of the same Opinion with them. And for this reason, God, who created us, and who knows what is most proper for us, hath ordained for our good, that all Particulars should be subject to the Authority of his Church, which, of all other Authorities, is without doubt the best established. In effect, it is established not only by that Testimony, which God himself gives of it in the Holy Scriptures, but also by the marks of his divine Protection, which are no less visible in the inviolable and perpetual subsistence of it, than in its miraculous Establishment. H SECT.

## SECT. XX.

*The Sentiments of those of the Pretended Reform'd Religion, concerning the Authority of the Church.*

THIS Supream Authority of the Church is so necessary to regulate the differences, which arise in matters of Faith, and about the Sense of Scripture, that our Adversaries themselves, after having decryed it, as an unsupportable Tyranny, have been at last obliged to establish it amongst themselves.

When those who are called Independents, declared openly, that each one of the Faithful ought to follow the light of his own Conscience, without submitting his Judgment to the Authority of any Body, or Ecclesiastical Assembly, and upon this ground refused to submit to any Synods; That of *Charenton* held 1644. censured this Doctrine upon the same Reasons, and for the same Inconveniencies, for which we reject it. This Synod observes in the first place, that
this

this Error of the Independents consists in this, that they teach, *Every Church ought to be governed by her proper Laws, without a dependance upon any Person in Ecclesiastical Matters, and without any Obligation to acknowledge the Authority of Conferences and Synods for her regulation and conduct.* After which this Synod determines, that this Sect is as prejudicial to the State as to the Church, that it opens a door to all sorts of Irregularities and Extravagancies; that it takes away all the means of applying any remedy to it; and that if it took place, there might be as many Religions framed as Parishes or particular Assemblies. These last words shew it is principally in matters of Faith, this Synod would establish a *Dependance*; seeing the greatest Inconvenience into which it observes the faithful would fall by an Independence, is, *that there might chance to be as many Religions formed as Parishes.* Every Church then (according to the Doctrine of this Synod) and much more every private Person, must necessarily depend, in what concerns matters of Faith, upon some o-

H 2     ther

ther superior Authority, which resides in some Assembly, or in some Body; to which Authority all the Faithful submit their Judgments. For the *Independents* do not refuse to submit to the Word of God, according as they think it ought to be understood; nor to accept the Decisions of Synods, when, after having examined them, they judge them reasonable. What they refuse to do, is to submit their Judgments to that of any Assembly for its sake; because our Adversaries have taught them, that every Assembly, even that of the Universal Church, is a Society of Men subject to Error, and to which, by consequence, a Christian ought not to submit his Judgment, that submission being only due to God. From this pretension of the *Independents* it is, those Inconveniences follow, which the Synod of *Charenton* so well observed. For, let a man make what profession he pleaseth to submit himself to the Word of God, if every one think he has a right to interpret it according to his own sense, and against the Tenets of the Church declared

*according to Protestants.*

declared in her last Sentence, this Pretension *will open a door to all sorts of Extravagancies*; it will take away all the means of applying a remedy; because the Decision of the Church is not a Remedy to those, who think themselves not obliged to submit to it; in fine, it gives way to the *framing as many Religions*, not only as there are Parishes, but also as there are Persons.

To avoid these Inconveniencies, from whence the ruin of Christianity would follow, the Synod of Charenton finds her self obliged to establish *a Dependence in Ecclesiastical Matters*, and that even in Points of Faith; but this dependence will never hinder those pernicious consequences which they desired to prevent, if they do not, with us, establish this Maxim, That every particular Church, and much more every particular Person amongst the Faithful, ought to believe themselves obliged to submit their private Judgment to the Authority of the Church.

Thus we see in the Fifth Chapter of the Discipline of the Pretended

Reform'd Religion, under the Title of *Consistories, Art. 31.* that going about to prescribe a Means to end *Debates, which might arise upon any Point of Doctrine or Discipline, &c.* they ordain first the Consistory shall endeavour *to appease the whole without noise, and with all the sweetness of the Word of God;* and after having established a Consistory, a Conference, and a Provincial Synod, as so many different degrees of Jurisdiction, coming at last to a National Synod, above which, amongst them, there is no Authority, they speak of it in these terms. *There the entire and final Resolution shall be given by the Word of God, to which if they refuse to acquiesce in every Point, and with an express disavowing of their Errors, they shall be cut off from the Church.* It is manifest those of the Pretended Reformation do not attribute the Authority of this last Sentence to the Word of God taken in it self, and without dependence upon the Authority of the Church; for tho this Word was made use of in their first Judgments, yet notwithstanding they

per-

*according to Protestants.*

permitted an Appeal. It is then this Word as interpreted by the Sovereign Tribunal of the Church, which gives *this final Resolution,* to which *whosoever refuses to submit in every Point,* altho he boast he is authorized by the Word of God, is no more reputed but as a profane Person who corrupts and abuses it.

But the Form of those Letters of Deputation which were address'd to the Synod of *Vitre* in the year 1517, to be observed by the Provinces when they were to send their Deputies to a National Synod, has yet something more express; it is in these terms. *We promise before God to submit our selves to all that shall be concluded and resolved of in your holy Assemblies, to obey them, and put them in execution to our utmost power, being perswaded, as we are, that God will preside in it, and lead you by his Holy Spirit into all Truth and Equity, by the Rule of his Word.* Here the Point is not about receiving the *Resolution* of a Synod, after they have found it to speak according to Scripture; they submit to it there even before it is assembled;

H 4

bled; and they do it becauſe they are perſwaded *the Holy Ghoſt will preſide in it.* If this Perſuaſion be only founded upon a Human Preſumption, can a man in conſcience *promiſe before God to ſubmit to all that ſhall be there concluded and reſolved of, to obey, and execute them to the utmoſt of his power?* And if this Perſuaſion has its foundation in a certain belief of the Aſſiſtance which the Holy Ghoſt gives to the Church in her final Deciſions, Catholics themſelves require no more.

So that the Proceedings of our Adverſaries ſhew them to agree with us in this Supreme Authority, without which it is impoſſible ever to put an end to any Difficulty in Religion; and tho, whilſt they were deſirous to caſt off the yoak of Obedience, they denied the Faithful to be obliged to ſubmit their Judgments to that of the Church, yet the neceſſity of eſtabliſhing an Order, has ſince forced them to grant what their firſt Undertakings had made them deny.

They have gone yet much further in the National Synod held at *St. Foy*
in

*according to Protestants.* 173

in the year 1578. There was some overture made of a Reconcilement with the *Lutherans*, by means of a general *Form of a Profession of Faith common to all their Churches*, which was proposed to be drawn up. Those of this Kingdom were invited to send to an Assembly, which was to be held upon this account, *Vertuous persons, authorised by all the said Churches, with an ample Procuration*, TO TREAT, AGREE UPON, AND DECIDE ALL POINTS OF DOCTRINE, *and other matters concerning that union*. Upon this Proposal, see in what terms the resolution of the Synod of St. Foy was couched. *The National Synod of this Kingdom, after having given God thanks for such an overture, and commended the care, diligence, and good advice of the forementioned persons convocated, and* APPROVING THE REMEDIES WHICH THEY HAVE SUGGESTED, that is to say, principally that of framing a new Confession of Faith, and to give power to some certain persons to compose it, has ordained, *That if the copy of*

H 5 *the*

*the above named Confession of Faith be sent in time, it shall be examined in each Provincial Synod, or otherwise, according to the convenience of each Province; and in the mean time has deputed four Ministers, the most experienced in those affairs, to whom express charge has been given to be present at the place and day appointed, with the Letters and full Procurations of all the Ministers, and Elders, Deputies of the Provinces of this Kingdom, as also of the Lord Viscount* Turenne, *to do all things above said: yea even, in case that* MEANS COULD NOT BE FOUND OUT TO EXAMINE IN EVERY PROVINCE THE SAID CONFESSION, *it should be referred to their prudence and sound judgment to agree and* CONCLUDE *all the points which shall be brought into deliberation, as well* FOR DOCTRINE, *as for other matters concerning the benefit, union, and peace of all the Churches.* It was to this, in fine, that this seeming tenderness of Conscience of these pretended Reformers tended. How often have they repreached to us, as a weakness, that

sub-

submission which we pay to the Decisions of the Church, which, say they, is nothing else but a company of men lyable to error? and yet nevertheless, being assembled in a Body in a National Synod, which represented all the Churches of the pretended Reform'd in *France*, they are not afraid, by mutual consent, to leave their faith to the arbitration of four men, with so absolute an abandoning of their own sentiments, that they gave them full power to change the very Confession of Faith it self, which they do at this very day propose to the whole Christian world as a Confession of Faith, which containeth nothing but the pure Word of God, and for which, as they said in presenting it to our Kings, an infinite number of people were ready to shed their Blood. I leave the prudent Reader to make his reflections upon the Decree of this Synod; and shall in a few words finish the Explication of the Churches Tenets.

SECT.

## SECT. XXI.

*The Authority of the Holy See of* Rome, *and of* Episcopacy.

THE Son of God, being desirous his Church should be one, and solidly built upon Unity, hath established and instituted the Primacy of St. *Peter* to maintain and cement it. Upon which account, we acknowledg this Primacy in the *Successors* of the Prince of the Apostles, to whom, for this cause, we owe that Obedience and Submission, which the Holy Councils and Fathers have always taught the Faithful.

As for those things, which we know are disputed of in the Schools, tho the Ministers continually alledg them to render this Power odious, it is not necessary we speak of them here, seeing they are not Articles of the Catholic Faith. It is sufficient we acknowledg a Head established by God to conduct his whole flock in his paths; which those who love Concord amongst Brethren, and Ecclé-

*Conclusion of this Treatise.*

clesiastical Unanimity, will most willingly acknowledg.

And certainly if the Authors of the Pretended Reformation had loved Unity, they would neither have abolished Episcopal Government, which was established by *JESUS CHRIST* himself, and which we find in force even in the times of the Apostles; nor have despised the Authority of *St. Peter's* Chair, which has so solid a Foundation in the Gospel, and so evident a succession in Tradition; but they would rather have carefully conserved Episcopal Authority, which establisheth unity in particular Churches, and the Primacy of *St. Peter's* Chair, which is the common Center of all Catholic Unity.

## SECT. XXII.

*Conclusion of this Treatise.*

THIS is the Exposition of the Catholic Doctrine, in which, that I might tye my self to the most principal, I have left some questions untouched, which those of the Pretended

tended Reform'd Religion do not look upon as lawful matter for a Separation. I hope those of their Communion, who shall impartially examin all the Parts of this Treatise, will be better disposed by the reading of it, to give ear to those proofs upon which the Faith of the Church is established, and will in the mean time acknowledg many of our Controversies may be ended by a sincere explication of our Tenets; that her Doctrine is Holy, and that, according to their own Principles, no one of her Articles destroys the grounds of Salvation.

If any one should think fit to answer this *Treatise*, he is desired to consider, that to accomplish his intent, he must not undertake to refute the Doctrine contained in it, seeing my Design was only to propose it, without going about to prove it; and that if in some Places I have hinted at some of the reasons which establish it, it is because the knowledg of the principal reasons of a Doctrine, is often a necessary part of it's Explication.

*Conclusion of this Treatise.*

It would also be a quitting of the design of this Treatise, to examin the different methods, which Catholic Divines make use of to establish or explicate the Doctrine of the Council of *Trent*, and the different Consequences, which particular Doctors have drawn from it. To urge any thing solid against this Treatise, and which may come home to the point, it must be proved that the Churches Faith is not here faithfully expounded, and that by Acts which the same Church has obliged her self to receive; or else it must be shown, that this Explication leaves all the Objections in their full force, and all the Disputes untouched; or, in fine, it must be precisely shown in what this Doctrine subverts the Foundations of Faith.

Letters

*Letters* and *Approbations* mentioned in the *Advertisement*.

A Letter from his Eminence the Card. BONA of happy Memory, to his Eminence the Card. de BUILLON.

HO ricevuto il libro di *Monsignor Vescovo di Condom*, che *V. E.* si è degnata inviarmi, e sì come Conosco la qualità del favore, e meno pregio, così rendo alla sua gentilezza infinite gratie e per il dono e per il pensiero che si prende di accrescere la mia Libraria. L'hò letto con attentione particolare, e perche *V. E.* mi accenna che alcuni lo accusano di qualche mancamento, hò voluto particolarmente osservare in che potesse esser ripreso. Mà realmente non sò trovarci se non materia di grandissima lode, perche senza entrare nelle questioni spinose delle controversie, con una maniera ingegnosa, facile, e famigliare, e con metodo, per così dire, geometrica da certi principii communi & approvati convince i Calvenisti, e li necessita à confessare la verità della' Fede Cattolica. Assicuro *V. E.* di haver lo letto con mia indicibile sodisfattione; nè mi maraviglio che gli babbino trovato à dire, perche tutte le Opere grandi, e che sormontano l' ordinario, sempre hanno contraditori. Vince però finalmente la verità, e da'frutti si connosce la qualità dell'albero. Me ne rallegrò con l' Autore, il quale hà dato saggio del suo gran talento con questa opera, e potrà con molte altre servire lodevolmente à Santa Chiesa. *Roma* 19. *Gennaro* 1672.

A Letter from his Eminence the Cardinal SIGISMOND CHIGI of happy Memory, to the Abbot of *Dangeau*.

RICEVEI con la sua lettera ill Libro della Espositione della Dottrina Cattolica del Vescovo di Condom, molto erudito e molto utile per convertire gl' heretici più con le vive ragioni, che con l'asprezza del discorso. Parlai al Padre, Maestro di S. Palazzo, & al Segretario dell' Congregatione dell' Indice, e conobbi veramente, che non viera stato chi havesse a questi Padri parlato in disfavore del medesimo. Anxi li trovai pieni di estimatione per il medesimo: & havendo poi parlato con questi Signori Cardinali della Congregatione, trovai

frà

frà gl'altri il Signor Cardinale Brancaccio molto inclinato a pregiarlo, e molto propensa a lodarne l' Autore. Onde io tengo certo che qua ancora Monsignor di Condom ottenga quella lode, che e dovuta alla sua fatica & alla sua dottrina. Resto per tanto obligato alla sua gentilezza che mi ha dato modo di ammirar la medesima; mentre mi pare che l' Autore stringa bene i suoi argomenti, e mostri chiaro i punti nei quali i divisi discordano della Chieza; ne credo che il modo che tien l' Autore, sia da condannarsi nell' esplicatione di qualche Dottrina insegnata dal Concilio di Trento, essendo praticato da molti Scrittori & essendo da lui maneggiato molto regolatamente; in oltre che l' Autore non ha havuto in mente d'interpretare i dogmi di quel Concilio; ma solo importarli nel suo libro esplicati perche gl'heretici restino convinti, & in chiaro di tutto quello che la Santa Chiesa gl'obliga di credere. Dell' autorità del Papa, ne parla bene, e con il dovuto rispetto della Sede Romana ogni volta che parla del capo visibile della Chiesa; onde torna à dire che non è capace che di lode. Roma 5. Apr.1672.

A Letter from the Rev. Father *HYACINTHUS LIBELLI*, at that time Master of the Sacred Palace, and now A. B. of *Avignon*, to the Card. *SIGISMOND CHIGI*.

HO letto il Libro del Sig. di Condom continente l' Espositione della Dottrina della Chiesa. Devo infinite gratie à V. E. che mi habbia fatte consumare quattro hore di tempo sì virtuosamente, e con tanto mio diletto. Mi è piacciuto sopra modo, e per l' Argomento singolare, e per le prove, che à quello corrispondono. La Dottrina è tutta sana ne v'ha ombra di mancamento. Ne per me sò quello che possa opporvisi; e se l' Autore desidererà che si ristampi in Roma, da me otterrà tutte le facoltà che gli saranno necessarie ad effetto che si ristampi senza mutarne ne pure una parola. L' Autore che ha molto ingegno si è servito in questa operetta del giuditio, perche lasciate da parte le dispute, che sogliono quasi sempre accrescer le discordie, trovandosi di raro chi voglia cedere le prerogative del ingegno al compagno, hà trovato un altro modo più facile

di

di trattar co' Calvinisti dal quale puo sperarsi maggior frutto. Perche ogni volta che perdin quel orrore à nostri dogmi che hanno succhiato col latte, à noi più volentieri s'accostano, e posta in malafede la dottrina che hanno apprefa da loro Maestri di cui la massima principale e essere i nostri dogmi orrendi & incredibili, si pongono con minor passion d'animo à cercar la verità Cattolica, che à quello a che devono esortarsi acciocche rineghino gli errori, perche, come V. E. discorreva l'atro giorno, la verità Cattolica vince appresso ogn' huomo prudente riconosciuta à petto dell' Eresia ogni volta che sia esaminata senza preoccupatione di spirito. Hò preso ardire di fare à V. E. questa lunga diceria per uno sfogo del contento, ch' hò havuto di legere il sudetto libro, che Ella hà fatto gratia di parteciparmi, e pregandola a continuarmi simili favori le bacio riverentemente le vesti. Roma, 26 Aprile 1672.

A Letter from the Bishop and Prince of *PADERBORNE* at that time Coadjutor, and now Bishop of *Munster*, to the Author.

QUANQUAM ad virtutem ac eruditionem tuam toti terrarum orbi omnique posteritati commendandam sufficiat judicium Regis Christianissimi, qui filium suum in spem tantæ fortunæ genitum tibi instituendum erudiendumque commisit: tu tamen immortali proprii ingenii monimento, aureo videlicet illo libello, cui titulus est, Expositio Doctrinæ Ecclesiæ Catholicæ, nomen tuum pariterque Christianam disciplinam magis illustrare voluisti; eoque non solum ab omnibus Catholicis maximos plausus tulisti, sed etiam ex ipsis heterodoxis verissimas ingenii atque doctrinæ tuæ laudes expressisti. Elucet enim in admirabili illo opusculo incredibilis quædam res difficiles & planè cælestes atque divinas explicandi facilitas, & gravissimus candor, ac verè Christiana Charitas atque Benignitas, qua sedentes in tenebris & umbra mortis tam suaviter allicis, & illuminas, ac dirigis in viam pacis, ut unus Episcoporum ad hostes Catholicæ fidei sub jugum suave veritatis mittendos factus & factus esse videaris. Quapropter ut eximii operis fructus longius manaret, atque per universam Germaniam, aliásque gentes sese diffunderet libellum tuum in latinum sermonem convertendi impetum cepi ; sed ubi literas tuas VIII. Cal. Maii datas perlegi, dubitavi sanè utrùm progredi oporteret, an incepto absistere, quia te non solùm Gallici, sed etiam Latini sermonis nitore ac elegantiâ tantopere pollere perspexi, ut quicunque præter temetipsum tua scripta de Gallico verteret, is pulcherrimum ingenii tui partum deformaturus potius, quàm ornaturus esse videretur. Quare tu potissimùm esses orandus, ut foetum, quem in lucem edidisti latinitate donares. Sed quia forsitan id tibi per occupationes non licet, & siquidem tantum tibi sit otii, obsecrandus es potiùs, ut plura scribas, quàm ut scripta convertas ; faciam id quod tibi pergratum esse significas, & illum cui hanc provinciam dedi urgebo, ut inchoata perficiat ; tibique versionem libelli tui censendam corrigendámque transmittam. Te verò, Præsul Illustrissime longéque doctissime, maximopere semper observabo & amicitiam tuam ad quam hic meus conatus & tua benignitas aditum mihi patefecit, omni officio colere studebo. Vale, Antistes eximie, ac de Republicâ Christianâ optimè merite, & me, ut facias, ama, atque Serenissimo Delphino cum optimis artibus atque præceptis nostram quoque memoriam & amorem instilla, & Ducem Montauserium meis verbis jube salvere plurimùm. In Arce meâ ad Confluentes Luppiæ, Paderæ & Alisonis, 3. Kal. Jun. 1673.

A Letter from the Rev. Father *RAIMUNDUS CAPISUCCHI*, Master of the Sacred Palace, to the Author.

IL merito sublime di V. S. Ill. da me ammirato, doveva esse ranche servito nell' occasione del dottissimo, & eruditissimo libro da lei composto in difesa della Fede Cattolica, & tradotto per beneficio di tutti anche nella Lingua Italiana, onde lo devo render singolarissime gratie, come faccio à V. S. Ill. dell' occasione, che mi hà dato di servirla. Stiamo tutti attendendo la publicatione di questo bellissimo libro, per godere delle sue nobilissime fatiche, & io in particolare che vivo, e vivero sempre

*sempre ambitioso di oltri suoi commandamenti, e qui per fine con ogni ossequio la riverisco.* Roma 20. Guign. 1675.

The Approbations of the Roman Edition Ann. 1678.

The Approbation of Signor *MICHEL ANGELO RICCI*, Secretary to the Congregation of I. and H. R. and Consultor of the Holy Office.

QUOD Tridentina Synodus magno studio assecuta est, ut doctrinam Fidei ab opinionibus, & controversiis inter Catholicos omninò secerneret, ac eandem apertiùs, & significantiùs explicaret; ac Tertullianus olim, ut Hæreticorum secessionem ab Ecclesia certis præscriptionibus improbaret; alii, ut principia quædem Hæreticorum, & regulas, ad refutationem ipsorum ingeniosè contorquerent: ea Clarissimus quoque Vir Jacobus Benignus Bossuet, Condomi Episcopus, præstitit in hoc Opere, perspicua methodo, brevi, & ad persuadendum accommodata, quæ quidem præclarum Auctoris ingenium refert. Quod Opus Italorum commoditati nunc eleganter versum è Gallica in maternam linguam prælo, ac luce dignum existimo. Romæ die 5. Augusti 1678.

*MICHAEL ANGELUS RICCIUS.*

The Approbation of the Reverend Father *LAURENCE BRANCATI DE LAUREA* of the Congregat. of Consist. I. Rites; Visit. Consultor and Qualificator of the Holy Office, and Bibliothecarian of the Vatican Library, &c.

LUCE dignum existimo Opusculum, seu discursum Gallicè & variis linguis impressum, nunc autem ex Gallico in Italicum idioma conversum, in quo Illustrissimus Dominus Jacobus-Benignus Bossuet Episcopus & Toparca Condomi, nobili, sed gravi ac solido stylo Religionis Prætensæ Reformatæ Ministros, & Asseclas, tam communibus Ecclesiæ fundamentalibus regulis, quàm propriis eorundem principiis fortiter perstringit, ostendens, non Catholicos, ut ii Ministri autumant, sed ipsosmet Ministros, per improprias consequentias recessisse ab Ecclesiæ dogmatibus,

*dogmatibus, nobis, ipsisque communibus; & ex pravis ejusmodi Scripturæ vel Conciliorum intelligentiis, Catholicam communionem reliquisse. Et si ipsi Ministri Catholicorum Regulas in Conciliis, præsertim in Tridentino fundatas, absque passione servarentur, proculdubio, ex Dei auxilio, ad sanctam redirent unitatem; & discurrens per singulas controversias suaviter, sed palmariè id exequitur. Datum in Conventu Sanctorum XII. Apostolorum. Romæ die* 25. *Julii* 1678.
*F. LAURENTIUS DE LAUREA MIN. CONVENTUALIS.*

The Approbation of the Abbot *Stephen Gradi.*

*LEGI diligenter, & studiosè egregium summi Viri Jacobi Benigni Condomensis Antistitis Opus, in sermonem Italicum fideliter elegamerque conversum, quo Doctrina Ecclesiæ breviter, enucleatè, luculenter exponitur. Indeque sic affectus animo discessi, ut legentes optima quæque, atque à sana doctrina, & summa ratione optimè paras, solent discedere, ut non alia se dicturos, nec aliter locuturos, si ad scribendum de talibus se contulissent, existiment. Super omnia verò me cepit Scriptoris, ut ita dicam, sobrietas in delectu rerum, quas promit, dum circumcisis, quæ lites extendere, & meliori causâ invidiam conflare nata sunt, ipsam veritatis arcem capessit, tutamque, & inaccessam præstat; totus in rectè constituendo controversiæ statu, quam ea re dijudicatu facilem, & expeditam efficit. Hunc itaque librum, si me audient, quibus concordi Ecclesiæ Christianæ, & salva sua ipsorum anima opus est, diurnâ nocturnâque manu versare non desinent; neque non fieri potest, ne eos diversa à Fide orthodoxa sentire non pigeat, pudeatque.*

Ita sentio ego STEPHANUS GRADIUS S. Congr. Indicis Consultor. & Biblioth. Vatic. Præf.

*Imprimatur si videbitur Reverendiss. P. S. P. Apost. Magistro.*

J. DE ANGELIS, Archiep. Urb. Vicesger.

*Imprimatur,* F. RAIMUNDUS CAPISUCCUS, Ord. Præd. S. P. A. Magister.

## The Breef of our Holy Father Pope *Innocent* the XI.

*Venerabilis Frater, salutem & apostolicam benedictionem.*
*Libellus de Catholicæ Fidei Expositione à fraternitate tua compositus, nobisque oblatus, ea doctrina eaque methodo ac prudentia scriptus est, ut perspicua brevitate legentes doceat, & extorquere possit, etiam ab invitis, Catholicæ veritatis confessionem. Itaque non solùm à nobis commendari, sed ab omnibus legi, atque in pretio haberi meretur. Ex eo sanè non mediocres in orthodoxæ Fidei propagationem, quæ nos præcipuè cura intentos ac solicitos, habet, utilitates redundaturas, Deo benè juvante, confidimus: ac vetus interim nostra de tua virtute ac pietate opinio comprobatur, magno cum incremento spei jampridem susceptæ fore ut institutioni tuæ creditus, eximia, hoc est paterna, avitaque præditus indole DELPHINUS, eam à te hauriat disciplinam, qua maximè informatum esse decet Christianissimi Regis filium, in quem unà cum florentissimo regno, Catholicæ Religionis defensio perventura est: idque perenni cum Regis ipsius decore, qui Fraternitatem tuam inter tot egregios viros, quibus Gallia abundat, ad opus potissimùm elegit, in quo publicæ fœlicitatis fundamenta jacerentur; cùm divino doceamur Oraculo, patris gloriam esse filium sapientem. Tu perge alacriter in incepto, ad quod incitare te, præter alia, magnopere debet, qui jam apparet laborum, atque industria tua fructus. Audimus enim & quidem ex omnium sermone, ac magno cum animi nostri solatio inter tot prementia mala audimus, DELPHINUM ipsum magno ad omnem virtutem impetu ferri, & paria pietatis atque ingenii documenta præbere. Illud tibi pro certo affirmamus, nulla in re devincire te arctiùs posse paternam nostram erga te voluntatem, quàm in regio adolescente bonis omnibus, & Rege maximè dignis artibus imbuendo, ut is adulta posteà ætate, Barbaras gentes & Christiani nominis inimicas, quas Parentem inclytum reddita Europæ pace, & translatis in Orientem invictis armis Imperio latè suo adjecturum speramus, victor & ipse sanctissimis legibus,*

*bus, moribusque componat. Devotionem interim atque observantiam quam erga sanctam hanc Sedem, nosque ipsos, qui in ea Catholicæ Ecclesiæ immerito præsidemus, tuæ ad nos literæ luculenter declarant, mutuæ charitatis affectu complectimur, cujus profectò in occasionibus quæ se dederint Fraternitati tuæ argumenta non deerunt, tibique Apostolicam benedictionem peramanter impertimur. Datum Romæ, apud S. Petrum sub annulo Piscatoris, die 4. Januarii 1679. Pontificatus nostri anno 3. MARIUS SPINULA.* And on the out-side, *Venerabili Fratri Jacobo, Episcopo Condomensi.*

The *foregoing* Testimonies rendred *English.*

*A Letter from his Eminence the Cardinal* BONA *of happy Memory, to his Eminence the Cardinal de*BUILLON.

I Have receiv'd the *R. Bishop of Condom's* Book, which your Eminence did me the Honour to send me; and as I am sensible of the Quality of this Favour, and esteem my self much honoured by it; so I render you my most cordial thanks, as well for the Present, as for the care you take to encrease my Library. I have read it with a particular attention; and because your E. tells me, there are some who find some fault in it, I endeavour'd expresly to observe in what it might be worthy of reprehension. But really I could not find any thing in it, but matter of great Commmendation; seeing, without entring into the more difficult Questions in Controversie, he makes use of a most

in-

ingenious, easie, and familiar manner, and of a Method, as I may say, Geometrical, to convince the *Calvinists* by common and approved Principles, and to force them to confess the Catholic Faith.

I can assure your E. I found, in reading it, a Satisfaction which I cannot express; and I am not astonished that some have found fault with it; for all Works great, and above the common level, find Persons still to contradict them. But Truth prevails in the End, and the quality of the Tree is known by the Fruit. I congratulate with the Author, who has by this Work given us an Essay of his great Talents, and may by many others render considerable Service to the Church.     *Rome, Jan.* 19. 1672.

*A Letter from Cardinal* SIGISMOND CHIGI, *of happy Memory, to the Abbot of* DANGEAU.

I Have received, together with your Letter, the Exposition of the Catholic Doctrine, compos'd by the Bishop of *Condom*. I have found it full of Erudition, and so much the more proper to convert Heretics, as it presses them with lively Reasons, without any Bitterness. I made mention of it to the Reverend Father, Master of the Sacred Palace, and to the Secretary of the Congregation *dell' Indice:*

*dice:* I understood that no body had spoken against it to these Fathers, who seemed to me, on the contrary, full of Esteem for this Work. I discoursed of it likewise to the Cardinals of the Congregation, and, amongst all the rest, I found Cardinal *Brancas* much enclined to praise the Author, and esteem the Book. So that I doubt not but *M. de Condom* will receive here the same approbation, which has been given him every where else, and which is so legitimately due both to his Learning, and his Labour. I am very much obliged to you for having given me the means of admiring him, and have perceived in this, your old and ordinary goodness. The Author is close in his Proofs, and explicates very clearly the Subject he treats on, in shewing the true difference betwixt the belief of Catholics, and that of the Enemies of the Church. I do not think the method he takes, to explicate the Doctrine taught in the Council of *Trent*, can in the least be disapprov'd; this Method having been practised by many other Writers, and being handled throughout his whole Book, with great Exactness. Certainly it was never his Intention to give the Interpretation of the Tenets of the Council, but only to deliver them in his Book, rightly explicated, in such sort that Hereticks may be convinc'd, and especially in those

I       things

things which the Holy Church obliges them to believe. He speaks perfectly well of the Popes Authority, and whereever he treats of the visible Head of the Church, he appears full of respect for the Holy See. In fine, I must tell you once again, *M. de Condom* cannot be too much commended, *&c. Rome, April* 5. 1672.

*A Letter from the Reverend Father* HYACIN-THUS LIBELLI, *at that time Master of the Sacred Palace, and now Archbishop of* Avignon, *to the Cardinal* SIGISMOND CHIGI.

I Have read *M. de Condom's* Book, which contains an Exposition of the Doctrine of the Church. I am extreamly indebted to your Eminence for giving me the opportunity of employing four hours so profitably, and with so much Pleasure. It is impossible for me to express how much this work has pleased me, both for the peculiar Excellence of the design, and for the Proofs which correspond to it. The Doctrine is found in all its parts; and without the smallest shadow of a fault. As for my self, I cannot see what can be objected against it; and if the Author would have the Book Printed at *Rome*, I will give all the necessary Approbations, without changing a single Word. This Author, who has a great deal of

Wit,

Wit, has shown a great deal of Judgment too in this Treatise, where, laying aside disputes, which ordinarily speaking do but encrease Dissentions, it being rare to find any who will grant the Preheminence of Wit to their Companions, he has found out another, and more easie, Method of treating with the *Calvinists*, from which much better Fruit may be expected. In effect, as soon as they can be brought to lay aside that horrour which they have sucked in with their Milk, against our Tenets, they come more willingly towards us, and discovering the insincerity of that Doctrine which they learn'd from their Masters, the principal Maxim of which is, That our Doctrines are horrid and incredible, they apply themselves, with more tranquillity of Mind, to search into Catholic Verities.

This is what they must be carefully exhorted to, since there is no better Method to make them renounce their Errors; and your Eminence had great reason when you lately said, That Catholic Truth will always be victorious in the Mind of every man of Sense, who will only without prejudice consider it in comparison with *Heresy*. I take the Liberty to write this long Discourse to your Eminence, not being able to contain within my self the Pleasure, which the reading of this Book, you have

J 2      been

been pleased to let me have, has afforded me. I beg your Eminence will continue the like Favours to me, &c. *Rome, 26 April, 1672.*

*A Letter from the Bishop and Prince of* PADERBORNE, *at that time Coadjutor, and now Bishop of* Munster, *to the Author.*

THE most Christian King, when he entrusted to you the Instruction and Education of his Son, born to so much Greatness, did by his Judgment alone sufficiently recommend your Knowledg, and your Merit to all the World, and all Posterity: yet you have given a new Lustre to your Reputation, and to the Christian Doctrine, by an immortal Monument of your Worth; I would say, by that most excellent Book, whose Title is, *An Exposition of the Doctrine of the Catholic Church*, which has not only gained the vast applause of Catholics, but forced the Hereticks themselves to give deserved Praises to your Judgment, and Erudition. In this most admirable Treatise, there appears a most incredible facility to unfold the most difficult, the most sublime, and most divine things; and at the same time a most winning candor, and a truly Christian Charity, and Bounty, capable to draw with sweetness all those who are set in Darkness, and in the shadow of Death, and to enlighten, and conduct

them

them into the way of Peace: Infomuch that you seem to be chosen amongst the Bishops, to reduce the Enemies of Catholic Faith under the easie Yoak of Truth. To the end therefore the effects of this great work might be the more extended, and might spread it self throughout all *Germany*, and amongst other Nations, I had formed to my self a design of having it put into *Latin*; but after having read your Letter of the 24th. of *April*, I had a doubt whether I ought to proceed any further in it, or quit my design, because I perceived you were as perfect a Master of the *Latin* Tongue, as of the *French*; and that you writ it with so much Purity, that if any other should undertake to translate your Works, instead of adorning those curious Products of your Wit, he might on the contrary discredit them. You ought the rather therefore to be desired to put what you have published your self in *Latin.* But seeing that perhaps you have not leisure, and, if you had, it would be much better you should be employed in the Composition of more new Works, than in the translation of those you have already Composed; because you admit of it, I will hasten him, to whom I have committed it, to finish what he has begun; and will send you the Version of your own Book, that you may review and correct it your self. What remains for me, is always infinitely to honour your Vertue and Learning, and to make it my endeavour to cultivate that Friendſhip, which my care of the Verſion, and your Bounty have given ſo favourable a beginning to. Continue ſtill to love me, moſt worthy Prelate, who ſerve the Church ſo well, and while you give the *Dauphin* ſo many excellent inſtructions, contrive for me a place in the remembrance and affection of ſo great a Prince. Give, if you pleaſe, my moſt humble Service to the Duke *de Montauſier*. In my Caſtle, at the Confluence of the *Lippe*, the *Padere*, and the *Aliſe*, the 29th. of *May*, 1673.

*A Letter from the Reverend Father* RAIMUNDUS CAPISUCCHI, *Maſter of the Sacred Palace, to the Author.*

After having admired with all others ſo ſublime a deſert as yours; I muſt alſo ſhew the particular Inclination I have to ſerve you, occaſioned by that excellent and learned Work you have compoſed for the defence of the Catholic Faith, and which has been lately tranſlated into *Italian*, for its farther ſpreading. I am indebted to you an infinite acknowledgment for having afforded me an occaſion of rendring you ſome Service; we are all of us here in great expectation of the publiſhing of

this

this excellent piece, that we may enjoy the fruits of your Labours. No body will have a greater satisfaction than my self, who do, and shall always feel an ardent desire to render my self worthy of the honour of your Commands. I end with assuring you of my Respects. *Rome*, 20 *June*, 1675.

## The Approbations of the *Roman* Edition, *Anno* 1678.

*The Approbation of Signor* MICHEL ANGELO RICCI, *Secretary to the Congregation of* I. *and* H. R. *and Consultor of the Holy Office.*

WHat the Council of *Trent* has with great care performed, in making an entire separation betwixt Articles of Faith, Opinions, and Disputes of the Schools; and explicating the same Doctrines of Faith in more clear and significant Terms; what *Tertullian* had formerly done, in condemning the departure of Hereticks from the Church by several Prescriptions; what others have practised, whilst they ingenuously combated Hereticks by their own Principles and Rules; the same has the Right Reverend *James Benign Bossuet* Bishop of *Condom* performed in this Work, in a clear and short Method, proper to perswade; manifesting to us the admirable parts of the Author.

Author. Which work being now for the convenience of the *Italians*, elegantly translated out of *French*, into our Mother Language, I esteem worthy to be Printed and Published. *Rome*, *August the 5th*. 1678.

*The Approbation of the Reverend Father* LAURENCE BRANCATI de LAUREA, *of the Congregat. of Consist. I. Rites; Visit. Consultor and Qualificator of the Holy Office, and Bibliothecarian of the* Vatican *Library*, &c.

I Esteem most worthy its being published the little Treatise or Discourse, Printed in *French* and several other Languages, and at present Translated out of *French* into *Italian*, in which the most Illustrious *James Benign Bossuet* Bishop and Lord of *Condom* does forceably combat in a Noble, Grave, and Solid Stile, the Ministers of the Pretended Reform'd Religion and their followers, as well by the common and fundamental Rules of the Church, as by their own Principles; showing, that it is not Catholics, as those Ministers imagine, but the Ministers themselves, who by drawing unnatural Consequences, have receded from those Tenets which are common to them and us, and by taking the Scriptures and Councils in a wrong sense, have separated themselves from

the

the Catholic Church. But if they would examin without paſſion the Rules of Catholics grounded upon their Councils, and eſpecially upon that of *Trent*, they would without doubt, by the Grace of God, return again to a Holy Unity: all which this Author ſhows them in a moſt pleaſing, and no leſs convincing manner, running through all the points of Controverſie. Given in the *Convent* of the Twelve Apoſtles at *Rome*, the 25. *July*, 1678.

F. *Laurentius de Laurea, Min. Conventualis.*

*The Approbation of the Abbot* Stephen Gradi.

I Have with diligence and application read the excellent Work of the Lord *James Benign Boſſuet*, Biſhop of *Condom*, faithfully and elegantly Tranſlated into *Italian*, where the Doctrine of the Church is explicated after a manner both conciſe, clear, and full. And it wrought the ſame Impreſſion in me, which ordinarily thoſe nobler ſort of Writings, which are the products of a ſound Doctrine and ſolid Reaſon, do in their Readers, when they are convinc'd they could not have ſaid any thing more to the purpoſe, nor ſpoken otherwiſe, if they had undertaken to write of the ſame Subject. But what Tranſported me the moſt was that Wiſdom and Moderation of the Author in the choice of thoſe things which he aſſerts; he retrenches

trenches all those things which serve only to lengthen Disputes, and render a good Cause odious, and betakes himself to Truth alone, as to a strong hold, which he renders not only secure but inaccessable: applying himself wholly to establish the true state of the Question, which by that means is rendred clear and easie to be judged of. Upon which account, all those, if they will believe me, who are concerned for the Peace of the Church, or the Salvation of their Souls, ought day and night to turn over this Book; and it is impossible, but it should produce in them both shame and sorrow, for holding Tenets, contrary to the Orthodox Faith.

I am of this Opinion,
    *St. G. Consultor* of the *Congregation de l' Indice*, *Prefect* of the *Vatican Library*.

Let it be Printed, if it so please the very Reverend Father, Master of the Sacred Apostolic Palace. *J. de Angelis Archiep. Urb. Vicesger.*

Let it be Printed,
  *F. Raimundus Capisuccus Ord. Præd. S.P.A. Magister.*

## The Brief of our Holy Father Pope Innocent XI.

VEnerable Brother, Health and Apostolical Benediction. Your Book of the *Exposition of the Catholic Faith*, lately presented to us, contains such Doctrine, and is composed in such a Method, and with so much Prudence, that it is thereby rendred proper to instruct the Readers clearly in few Words, and to extort, even from the unwilling, a Confession of the Catholic Faith. For which Reasons we do not only think it worthy our Commendation, but also to be read and esteem'd by all. We hope, this Work, by the Grace of God, will bring forth much Fruit, and will not a little help to propagate the Orthodox Faith, which is our continual Care, and principal Sollicitude. And in the interim, we are more and more confirmed in that good Opinion we have always had of your Vertue and Piety, and we feel an increase of those Hopes which we had long since formed in our selves, of the Education of the *Dauphin* of *France*, and that he who is intrusted to your Care, and endowed with Inclinations worthy the King his Father, and all his Ancestors, will receive from you those Instructions which are proper to the Son of a most Christian King, whose Birth entitles him both to so flourishing a Kingdom, and at the same time to be a Protector of the Catholic Religion. And this King, who has chosen you amongst so many Great Men, with which *France* flourishes at this time, to so great a Province, as is the laying the Foundations of a Public Happiness, will no doubt receive an Eternal Glory from the good Success of your Care, according to that Oracle of Scripture, which tells us, *That a wise Son is the Glory of his Father*. Continue then to go forwards chearfully in so important a Work, especially since you have before your Eyes such mighty Fruits of your Industry. For we hear, and that

*from*

from all Parts, and we cannot but feel an excess of Jo
and Consolation, amidst our many Troubles, when w
hear, how this young Prince is carried on to Vertue with
a noble Fervour, and daily gives new Testimonies o
Prudence and of Piety. This we can assure you, tha
nothing is capable of endearing our Paternal Affection
to you more, than thus to employ your utmost Care to
inspire into this young King's Mind those Maxims which
make a mighty King; that in a riper Age, being happy
and victorious, like the King his Father, he may regulate
by Holy Laws, and reduce to Christian Manners, Barbarous Nations, and Enemies of the Name of *Christian*
as we hope to see them shortly subdu'd to the Empire
of this Great King, since Peace being restored to *Europe*,
he has so fair an opportunity to transfer his Victorious
Arms into the *East*. To conclude, Assure your self, the
Submission and Respect which your Letters show you to
have towards the Apostolic See, and Us, who now possess it, tho unworthy, for the Government of the Catholic Church, find in Us a mutual Affection; the Testimonies of which, you shall perceive, when any occasion shall present it self. With a sincere Affection we give
you our Apostolic Benediction. Given at *Rome*, at *St.
Peters*, under the Fishers Ring, the 4th. of *January*,
1679. the Third year of our Popedom. Signed *Marius
Spinula*; and on the out-side, *To our Venerable Brother*,
James *Bishop of* Condom.

*FINIS.*

www.ingramcontent.com/pod-product-compliance
Lightning Source LLC
Chambersburg PA
CBHW020922230426
43666CB00008B/1538